Kids' rooms

ROCKPORT

First published in the United States of America by
Rockport Publishers, Inc.
33 Commercial Street
Gloucester, Massachusetts 01930-5089
Telephone: (978) 282-9590
Facsimile: (978) 283-2742
www.rockpub.com

ISBN 1-56496-771-9

10 9 8 7 6 5 4 3 2 1

Design: Nicole Curran
Production and layout: *tabula rasa*
Front cover image: Paul Whicheloe
Back cover images: Laura Ashley (top); Tim Street-Porter (middle)
All featured crafts courtesy of Craftopia.com
Bathroom tile photos by Sandy Levy, courtesy of Terry Tiles, Miami, FL

Printed in China.

GLOUCESTER MASSACHUSETTS

Kids' rooms

A HANDS-ON DECORATING GUIDE

ROCKPORT PUBLISHERS

Anna Kasabian

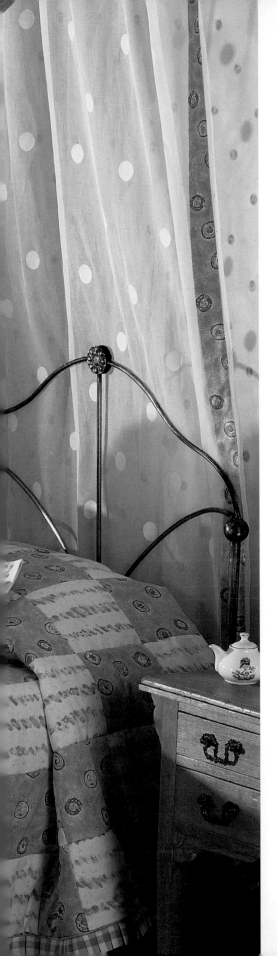

CONTENTS

FOREWORD

As you begin to design your child's room and the family spaces in your home, think first about the job your house has to do and your power to enable it to do so. Plan for comfort, peace, quiet, flow, privacy, inspiration, and the safety of the nest.

In researching this book, I asked *Parent* magazine's managing editor, Mary Mohler, the mother of three teenagers, what she thought of getting children involved in the design process. She thinks it's a good idea but points out that older children should have a greater voice than younger kids, who need more limits. After all, the four-year-old who really, really wants a bed shaped like a horse may prefer a cow tomorrow.

To begin the design dialog, Mary suggests asking your child broad questions: What is your favorite color? What animals do you like? What do you like to do the most?

Then get more specific: Would you like to have a fish or a zebra on this wall?

No *carte blanche,* she warns, as preferences can be elaborate. To a reasonable extent, however, you can honor requests, weaving visuals or activity centers into the room.

Mary observes that, by age four, children communicate their likes and dislikes and, by seven, are influenced by their peers. Thus, at seven, children like a major redesign of their room. That's when, for Mary's children, a globe, a personal computer, and bookshelves became important elements.

Overall, her advice is to work with your children and, in the end, purchase what you can live with.

Storage is an important planning focus. Work it in wherever you can. If children share a room, remember to respect their need for privacy. Give each a place to put precious possessions. Consider setting up an alcove for each child or installing a room divider.

Family spaces should be comfortable and easy to clean. One should feel free to put one's feet on the coffee table, and it should be okay for these rooms to look a little messy. Being caught up in how your house looks—especially where everyone gathers to enjoy each other's company—is a turnoff to kids and also, I believe, stunts communication. After all, aren't homes places to convene?

Above all each home should have a room where all family members can do things together. It can include a quiet corner for reading and doing crafts. Such places encourage talking while sharing an activity, like playing checkers.

Embrace this design adventure. Your children's rooms are gardens for their imagination and their dreams.

INTRODUCTION

Often, as I wrote this book, I thought of rooms I ventured into as a child—the homes that welcomed me. I even recalled the mouse family house my father described in bedtime stories. All the rooms and houses I spent time in colored my life—little watercolor scenes always being added to.

The rooms I played and slept in, at the homes of friends and relatives, surfaced. One of my favorites was my Aunt Josie and Uncle Frank's house. I loved its bigness and the massive staircase that curved to the top landing. My cousins and I slid down the banister often. We ran down the wide halls playing cowboy. This house was welcoming and fun, like a big play area. No rules, no fuss from my aunt.

Kids' Rooms

Down the street was my Aunt Lena and Uncle Phil's home, full to the brim with five children. The dining room table became a great cave for us, and the knotty pine basement was where we played games. Its long storage closet was a secret passage to the other side of enemy lines. Bedrooms were on the top floor, and I loved the way the windows were tucked under the eaves. My cousin Marilyn's window faced the front yard. Her brothers' room was an architectural twin, except it had built-in drawers on two sides. I loved the coziness of those rooms.

Then there was my friend Ellen's house—for me, right out of a storybook. It is a big, wooden clapboard farmhouse with a circular driveway and big lawn. Ellen's room was my dream come true. Its big canopy bed was dressed with beautiful white linens. The closet was the most magnificent ever; it was like a little room, with built-in drawers and shelves.

Your home and the rooms within are paints for your children's memories—a great, great gift to give them.

My goal is to bring you much more than a collection of attractive rooms that only a designer could produce. I want to help you create rooms yourself, to provide visuals that you can adapt as needed.

I also want you to hear children's thoughts. They talk here, with the purest honesty, about what they wish they had in their rooms and will, no doubt, fertilize your design garden. In addition, I include children's drawings of their ideas and offer ways with which you can translate their designs.

In addition, you will meet four families, and get tips from parents.

Finally, I include craft projects and tips, all with the hope that you can make your nest a place you and your children enjoy.

I hope I can help you talk with your children and think of ways to make them a part of the design process. I believe, in the end, lessons can be learned that go beyond design.

MAKING ROOM

INFANTS

The best way to develop a design plan for an infant's room is to think through the big picture of your family life. Is this room likely to be used by the same child for several years, or will it always be the new baby's room?

If your family is growing and this is the first of several children you plan to have, consider designating it the infant's room. This way, you need to decorate and furnish it only once for at least a few years. For flexibility, choose yellow as a main color, and keep decorations themed to accommodate both boys and girls.

You will spend a lot of time in your baby's room, so in planning it, take into account your activities, style of organization, and the everyday needs of babies. Infants use bedrooms mainly for sleeping and having diapers and outfits changed. You'll be going in and out of here a lot, tending to these tasks, so storage, lighting, and flooring must be carefully considered.

If possible, choose a room that is not too far from your bedroom so that late-night feedings and diaper changes can be attended to quickly without disrupting the rest of the family. Also, you'll be glad not to run down a long hall or climb stairs when you've just woken up.

In addition, if you've got the luxury of space, choose a room away from where your toddlers sleep. A new baby's fussing can be disruptive.

This chapter on infants' rooms will help you think through design options and offer tips on choosing a theme and accessorizing.

Opposite: Remember how much time you will spend here when you select wallpaper and furnishings. This room's soft, subtle floral wallpaper will not get stale, and it's set up with pleasing reminders that your daughter will soon be at the table playing! Notice the rocker; you will want one for late-night feedings.

Above: Create a fantasy room for yourself and your baby. Here, a soft mint green pastel dominates, and a decorative wall painting suggests a forest. The trees and animals on the walls are accented with bunting and a little painted table; both express the nature theme.

How to Choose a Theme

Before making any design decisions, consider whether or not this room will remain the new baby room. If it will, you should definitely invest in well-made, sturdy furnishings rather than trendy, less durable styles. Likewise, select a theme that will endure, be suitable for both boys and girls, and be pleasing to you. After all, you will be in and out of this room, day and night, for many months.

On the other hand, if this will remain your child's room for several years, choose design options that can easily make the transition from infant to toddler to perhaps a seven-year-old with minimal expense.

Ask yourself these questions:

- What kind of chair would be best for rocking the baby?
- When I greet the baby in the morning, sun streaming through the windows, what colors and patterns will make me feel happy?
- What can be added to the walls and floors for me and the baby to talk about?

Many design choices are available. To come to the right decision, think about themes in broad terms:

- **Fantasy:** This kind of room takes you to a new place and time. It may have nothing to do with the rest of the home's decor. The crib may be surrounded with a tent of fabric, ribbons, and bows, for example, and may remind you of a romantic story you read once. Practicality is not in this room plan!
- **Ultramodern:** This room takes advantage of all that is sleek, clean, and contemporary. Furnishings have simple lines and the palette is in subtle shades of white, off-white, and cream. Carry the theme to the walls and adorn them with black-and-white photographs framed simply in black or white wood. Wallpaper might be simple—perhaps elegant angel wings that accent one wall or a portion of a wall.

Above: Notice how the bunnies and other little creatures carry onto the lampshade, soaps, and other decorative items. These little setups are nice and soothing for both you and your baby to look at.

Opposite: Take a traditional design path and use wallpaper with a storybook theme. This approach allows easy accessorizing. Also, with all-white furniture and window treatments, other fabrics can be introduced that hold to the palette.

- **Antique:** Taking this route offers lots of design possibilities and period themes, from colonial to French country to Victorian. Bureaus, chairs, and armoires can anchor the theme, and accessories like antique photos, floor lamps, and quilts enhance it. Follow through with wall paint as well as wallpaper. Many companies reproduce period colors and patterns.
- **Traditional:** Visuals like storybook characters, farmyard scenes, or children at play make their way into these rooms via fabric, wallpaper, rugs, hand-painted furniture, and even lampshades. Furniture styles that work nicely here vary from white woods to naturals.

The next job is to think about how to incorporate a theme. The possibilities are myriad. Keep in mind the length of time the room will be used by the child—infancy only or on through toddlerhood. Here are some options for versatile, budget-conscious design:

- Use a washable wallpaper pattern to introduce lots of pattern. For a nature theme with puppies or kittens, mix and match the paper with complementary colors. This is appropriate in both bedroom and bath.
- Try decorative painting on the walls, ceilings, or floors—or both. A storybook theme on the curtains could be reinforced by continuing a visual via paint.
- Express the theme on only the window treatments for easy changing.
- Cover only the ceiling in wallpaper! Sky patterned wallpaper makes a dreamy effect.
- Carry over visual themes in blankets, bunting, pillows, and upholstered furniture.
- Complement a theme with painted furniture. Bookcases, a table and chairs, and toy chests are all good candidates.

Above: Neutral walls and striped wallpaper with a subtle theme make it easy to alter this room when baby grows into boy. For the baby, the bunting carries the visual theme of knights; curtains in the same design will work fine for the toddler.

- Paint the upper portion of walls of the room and use themed wallpaper on the lower half. This makes changing the theme easier.
- Paint the walls a plain pastel color. Add an artistic pattern or mural to the ceiling.
- Use complementary colors on the walls and window borders. Introduce themes only on fabrics.
- Use wallpaper with stripes or another geometric form. Suggest that this is a baby's or young child's room with accessories like stuffed animals and hanging quilts.
- Use plain, checked, or striped fabric to frame windows; use hooks to drape it over each side of the window. To save money, buy one piece of fabric and hem it yourself with sewing tape. For an elegant look, buy extra fabric and let it pool on the floor. Use shades to darken the room. When it's time for a change, use the fabric to cover pillows or make a playroom tent.
- Use any fabric theme on a window shade to keep the decor very flexible and easy to change.
- Keep walls and curtains white. Introduce color and themes in the accessories.
- Choose a broad theme that's easy to live with, like the sky, or a simple theme, like the outdoors or the beach, that can repeat in interesting ways.

Whether you decide to paint the walls, use wallpaper, or do a little of both, remember that you want to step into this room and feel relaxed (even if you're not!), and you want your baby to feel soothed as well. The idea here is to avoid overstimulation. That's not to say scenes of children playing outside should be avoided, but it might be a good idea to investigate wallpaper scenes that look like soft watercolor creations.

Above: There are many ways to bring a theme together. In this room, the teddy bear is repeated on the quilt, sleepwear bag, curtains, and a portion of the wallpaper. Since the major part of the wallpaper has flowers, butterflies, and geometric shapes, the theme can be changed easily and inexpensively.

Themes and Places to Carry Them Out

Consider choosing simple white or natural wood cribs and bureaus for the greatest freedom to work a theme, build a palette, and use the most options in fabric patterns. If you have family heirloom furnishings, don't worry about mixing eras. An antique bureau that belonged to your great-grandmother can work beautifully with a simple wooden crib. Use old family pieces, from your grandfather's train set to your mom's high chair as design elements. They'll provide eye-catching pools of history—things you can talk to your child about someday.

Here are some ways to weave a theme through your baby's room if antiques are the focus (many of these suggestions pertain to new items as well):

- Frame old postcards that align with the theme, and cluster ten or so on a wall.
- Line up antique toys, from fire engines to dolls, on a single shelf that surrounds the room.
- Hang an antique quilt that shares the palette or theme on the wall.
- Display antique children's clothing and other interesting pieces on the walls on antique hangers.

If the theme is babies at the beach, consider these options:

- Devote a portion of a wall to a display of toddler-size sand buckets and shovels.
- Paint the floor of the room to look like water and sand. Paper the lower half of the walls with colorful fish.
- Create a beach-themed lampshade by gluing shells around the edge of a plain shade.
- Use fabric that depicts a beach theme, or keep it simple and go with soft, pastel-striped cotton for curtains and pillows.

Above: Consider putting antique heirlooms into your baby's room. The exquisite details on this marble-topped Victorian chest of drawers really stand out in the nearly all-white room. The blue-and-white hand-painted blocks on the hardwood floor also help the chest stand out and complement the other touches of blue.

Right: The curtain detailing adds a nice touch.

Above: Here's a good idea for a little girl's room. Use striped wallpaper and border it with the alphabet. This is a theme with staying power.

Supporting Accessories

The basics are discussed above. Enhance the theme by introducing accessories in the same palette or with complementary pictures. Here is a checklist of possibilities:

- stuffed animals
- posters (antique or new)
- clothing racks
- rugs
- clothing bags
- hampers
- lamps
- prints

- bookends
- night-lights
- toy chests
- clocks
- books
- photos
- paintings

Above: Here is an inexpensive way to accessorize using colorful wall art, stuffed animals, and a few standing sculptures. Changing this room from a baby's to a four-year-old's would require neither papering nor painting.

Left: Ready-made patterns can be matched with ease; many retailers offer coordinated linens and curtains, fabric, wallpaper, and quilts.

UNEXPECTED **DECORATING IDEAS**

Design themes come in many forms, and they certainly do not have to be composed of the usual elements we know all too well. Here are fresh ideas for thinking outside the "design box."

Use **music boxes and music** as a **theme.** For example, antique or new music boxes can play sweet lullabies on your baby's bookshelves while you maintain the music theme with wallpaper or decorative painting (put multicolored notes all around the room or paint the words to a lullaby on the floor). Frame old or new music sheets of classic baby songs.

Go to flea markets and generate a small collection of baby dishes. Display them on shelves or hang them on the walls. Create a mobile with old **silver** baby feeding **spoons** and hang it near a window. When the breeze comes by, the spoons will ring.

Introduce a mommy tree on the wall. Incorporate as many **photographs of mommies** as you can find. Frame them in different-colored frames, or purchase unpainted frames and make decorating them a family project.

Sprinkle **mirrors** of different sizes and shapes around your baby's room. These are not only decorative but handy for pointing, talking, and distracting, when necessary.

A **PARENT** CORNER

Create a little corner for yourself in your baby's room, as a survival kits of sorts. When the baby is ill or fussy and alert to your presence in the room, a parent corner makes it easier for you to rock and read at the same time. Then, when the baby calms down and silence sets in, the quiet will let you relax a little, too.

For example, if you have a **rocker** in your baby's room, add a **side table** stocked with reading materials for yourself. If space permits, include a little **footstool** so you can rest, too.

Here are **other items** to consider leaving in a parent corner:

- an extra pair of reading glasses
- a book of poetry, a novel, magazines
- a reading light
- a little sewing or knitting project
- stationery and a pen
- loose photos and an album

Don't be caught by surprise; make a budget for your baby's room.

Do some homework so your design budget is realistic. Look through flyers and magazines, search furnishing sites on the Internet, and check costs for cribs, bedding, lamps, accessories, paint, and wallpaper.

If this task seems overwhelming, consider hiring an interior designer for an hourly fee to help develop a budget and make suggestions. Should you choose to do this on your own, make a list of mandatory furnishings— for example, crib, changing table, and rocking chair. Estimate their cost based on your research. Subtract that from the budget and see what's left for wallpaper, paint, carpeting, window treatments, and accessories like lamps, bookshelves, and incidental furnishings.

DECORATING **TIPS FROM A PRO**

Esther Sadowsky of Charm & Whimsy, Manhatten, New york, is an interior designer specializing in creating murals and custom-designed furniture for children's rooms. She designs everything from beds to lamps. Following are her tips on how to design and think about your child's space.

Make an overall plan before you buy: Clip photos of rooms, accessories, and color palettes that appeal to you; get samples from a fabric store; measure the dimensions of the room, including doors and windows; know your budget.

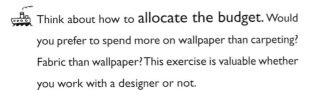 Think about how to **allocate the budget.** Would you prefer to spend more on wallpaper than carpeting? Fabric than wallpaper? This exercise is valuable whether you work with a designer or not.

If the budget is tight but you would like some help, work with a **retail store** to outfit your child's room.

Purchase extra fabric so as the room changes, you can **use the old theme in new ways**—to cover a comforter, for example. You can get the same fabric later, but it won't match perfectly.

Dry-clean fabrics for less fading. Dry-clean fabrics together for even treatment.

Remember that carpet fades over time. Think about this when you **place the crib,** which will eventually be replaced by the bed.

Allow some **space for play** and **creativity,** and include blackboards and bulletin boards.

 To **avoid worry about spills and stains,** consider a few vinyl furniture coverings. Successful examples include window seat cushions and diaper changing pads. For rugs, use a fiber seal.

Consider a **flat-weave carpet** so toy trucks and cars can roll easily and puzzles can be assembled. Avoid sisal—too rough on the skin!

A bare floor is cold for kids. When you run in at midnight, you will appreciate **carpeting,** too.

Flexible lighting is important. Table lamps are fine, but if you're renovating, put sconces over the crib on a dimmer so you can feed the baby in the middle of the night.

DECORATING TIPS
FROM THE KIDS

Samantha

When I asked Samantha what her favorite part of her room was, she barely hesitated before choosing her stuffed animals. Here she drew one of her favorites, and she surrounded it with two others, just to make her design point! She held true to the colors and shapes that make up the stuffed animals, too.

Here are ideas for bringing elements of Samantha's drawing into a room design project:

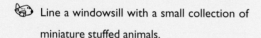 Line a windowsill with a small collection of miniature stuffed animals.

Hunt for wallpapers, wallpaper borders, and accessories like lampshades, bed covers, curtains, and rugs with an animal theme.

Note the colors in the drawing and see how they might work in the room. A solid hot-pink rug on a painted yellow floor could make for an exhilarating roomscape!

Explore other ways to bring the stuffed animal theme into the room—perhaps a rug shaped like an animal. For example, Samantha has a white throw rug in her sitting room that resembles a dog.

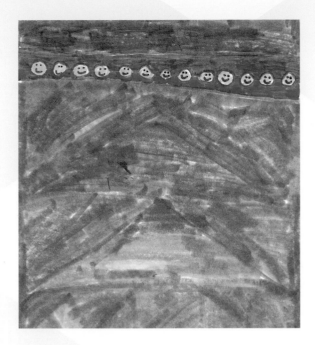

Jennifer

I asked ten-year-old Jennifer to draw what she would like for wallpaper in her room, and she came up with this. Posing this question to your child can give you a good idea of what colors and shapes appeal and can jump-start a face-lift plan. I want to emphasize that this exercise can be offered as an idea for fun—not an absolute guarantee that the drawing will become the wallpaper.

"I want to **paint the walls** a dark color, have a **smiley-face border** in wallpaper, and then a **silver trim** that looks red one way and silver the other. I'd like a **bedspread** the same as the wall. The walls would have band **posters** on them."
—Jennifer, age 10

Here are ways to translate Jennifer's lead drawing into a room design. Note that purple is the color of choice, so if you think it can work, explore ways to weave it into the room or make it the predominant color.

Paint the walls pale lavender and the trim in a deeper purple. The darker color could work perfectly in an easy-to-clean, semigloss latex finish. Alternatively, paint the ceiling deep purple.

Find existing accessories that feature the smiley face—rugs, lampshades, etc.

Adapt the design idea to window treatments that you and your daughter make together. Sew a purple curtain and have your child cut smiley faces from yellow fabric and eyes and smiles from black. Sew the faces onto a band of fabric and sew the band to the purple curtain.

Develop a room with these colors as the base, and use the smiley faces as a pillow treatment. Buy pillows and make your own smiley face covers—you've taken the idea to a new place.

Here are some ideas for incorporating Nicole's ideas into the design of her room:

🐟 Because Nicole is a young girl whose interests may change quickly, covering part of a wall in her room with blackboard would be an appealing, flexible way to encourage her creativity. She can then change her "wallpaper" whenever she wishes.

🚢 A good range of colors is presented here—from orange and pink to brown and green. Consider using green on the floor, through either carpet or paint, to bring the playing field inside.

🔆 Sports equipment could be stored in woven baskets, in a sports net hung on the wall, or on shelving. Nicole's parents could paint unfinished shelves with her favorite colors (they can always be repainted!) and add sports-themed decoupage to the shelves and edges.

🥧 Sheets, blankets, and curtain fabric can also be introduced with a sports theme.

Nicole

Nicole is Jennifer's younger sister. The six-year-old decided to develop wallpaper with a sports theme. If her mom liked this idea, she could start a new room design by exploring existing wallpapers and fabrics that focus on sports—to see if any would work in Nicole's room.

"I would paint the walls a **darkish blue** and have a border with **sports** stuff. I like bunk beds because I'll be able to reach my radio. I'll keep my Pooh Bear sheets, but I'd like to put sticky **stars on the ceiling,** and I would like to plant two sunflowers, too."

—Nicole, age 6

My teddy bear

Marcella

Nine-year-old Marcella quickly drew three things that matter to her. She produced a big yellow pillow with her initial on it, her teddy bear, and a wallpaper pattern that she would love in her room.

Marcella's wallpaper pattern could be easily accomplished with a wall of blue paper and a border of little flowers. This could work in the bedroom and in a bathroom as well, if she has her own. The flowers could become part of a bigger theme and touch her linens, blanket, rugs, or wall art.

Here are some ways to interpret Marcella's designs and items:

- The yellow-and-red pillow and the teddy bear with a hint of red on his ears suggest a soft and cuddly theme to carry out via piles of pillows on the bed and, perhaps, a chair.

- The monogram could become a design element. Marcella could learn to sew and monogram items in the room herself. Kits are available to help with this. Parent and child could enjoy sharing this hobby.

- The teddy bear suggests a bear or broader animal theme. The latter could evolve into a circus theme, opening the possibility of faux painting or floor painting design projects.

- Continue the animal theme by covering a number of pillows with different fabrics printed with bears, elephants, leopard patterns, or jungle scenes.

DESIGN GETS REAL

AT LILI BAO LAN'S HOUSE

What makes a perfect room for kids is far from an exact science. For real-life answers to creating kid-friendly design with style and savvy—I turned to four families for ideas and inspiration. You'll find them profiled here, and through the rest of the book. Although no two children are the same, and each family has a completely unique background and approach, I hope that their collective creativity will give you rich possibilities for making kid smart designs of your own.

At 16 months, LiLi Bao Lan has taken over major portions of her old country cottage home, but the parents of this ever-smiling baby—whose name means precious orchard—don't mind one bit. Their house has trails of toys and books from the living room to the kitchen. Even in the dining room, a chandelier detailed with hanging bunny eggs makes a clever distraction on the walk to the breakfast table.

Of course, simple safety alterations have made the home more LiLi-friendly, but perhaps the best alteration is her parents thoughtful approach to decor that embraces their little girl's presence in every room. The living room—a grouping of comfortable seats—is pushed back, out of this energized baby's path; her toys are here and there, ready for her hand or inquisitive eye's focus. At this age, too, the

need for multiple distractions is obvious, so the room is well stocked!

Fireplace pokers are hidden behind chairs; table lamps are retired and small decorative accessories are stored away. Lili's mom, Katherine, decided to leave photos out, however, so that as LiLi moves about, she can play Who's That? with her parents.

In the kitchen, the silver items and platters that once added color to the open

shelves were replaced with LiLi's drinking cup and toys. Under the work island is more LiLi turf—a big basket filled with plastic eggs and a whisk so she can pretend to help cook.

LiLi's bedroom walls are painted a soft, soothing blue-gray and green with a polka-dot pattern. The sheer curtains in the two sunny windows have pockets designed into them—the perfect solution for bedtime blues, as LiLi can listen to stories about the stuffed animals tucked into the pockets.

Other basic design elements include a crib, a bureau (which belonged to her grandparents and was painted white to match the crib), a changing table (with drawers that hold not only skin essentials but also toys to distract her while she's being changed), a rocking chair (a consignment shop find), and bookshelves, which are conveniently tucked behind the chair.

For safety's sake, hard, unbreakable toys are on the lower shelves, surrounded by soft stuffed animals. Books are stored higher so LiLi cannot pull them down, but when she's in the rocker with Mom, she can see the books and choose the day's reading.

The crib came with the Laura Ashley bedding from a consignment shop, and that set the palette. "We were going to do the room in bright colors with punches of peony pink and orange until we saw this," Katherine notes.

In the end, they introduced pink by painting the ceiling, trimming the mirror in pink ribbon, adding a pink cover to the changing table, and accessorizing with boxes, small toys, and lampshades.

Two little hats hang on the wall; LiLi loves to wear the one that comes from China. A scroll behind the rocker displays her name in Chinese characters.

When LiLi grows out of her crib, a twin bed will fit nicely in the space, and the toys in the curtain pockets will be replaced with more age-appropriate items. "With no rabbits on the walls, this is the kind of a room that would appeal to someone who doesn't want to be locked into a design motif," says Lili's mom.

MATERIALS

Polymer Modeling Clay, 2 oz.:
5 white, 3 translucent, 3 pearl

Waxed paper

Rolling pin

Rubber alphabet stamps

Pencil

Assorted sea shells

Glass baking dish

Super glue

CRAFTING WITH KIDS

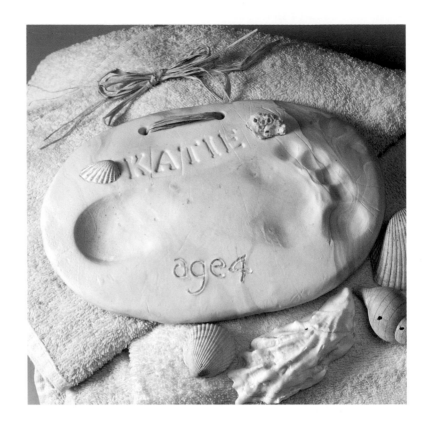

SEASIDE MEMORY PLAQUE

Children love toys and accessories made especially for them.
A mom-crafted item in your child's room will provide the personal touch that tells a child she's special while enhancing a
decorative theme. In each chapter we include simple craft projects and step-by-step instructions for decorative furnishings to
spice up children's rooms. Involve older kids in the craft projects to add to their pride of place and sense of achievement,
and for rainy day fun that lasts.

Create this faux marble plaque with polymer clay and alphabet stamps. Add a child's footprint and some pretty shells, and you have a permanent memento of your beach vacation. A quick trick—briefly microwave the clay to soften it and add a footprint. Collect shells, pretty stones, or even small bits of driftwood on your next trip to the beach, and use them to decorate the plaque around the footprint.

INSTRUCTIONS

1. Knead two or three clay blocks of one color together until softened. Repeat for each color until you have kneaded all the clay and softened it. Make long fat logs of each color, and lay them next to each other on waxed paper. Twist the logs together. Fold the twisted piece in half. Roll it into another log and twist it to marbelize the colors. Roll the clay into a tight oval-shaped ball. Make sure that the ball is tight and there are no air bubbles in it. Roll the ball between two sheets of waxed paper with a rolling pin, until you have a plaque about .5" (1 cm) thick and approximately 8.5" (22 cm) long by 6" (15 cm) wide.

2. Place the plaque on a paper towel and microwave on medium for one minute at a time until warm and soft to the touch. Make sure the clay is not hot. Then have a child press a foot into the clay, making an imprint. Use alphabet stamps to imprint the child's name above the footprint. Use a pencil or a bamboo skewer to write the age. Press shells or stones into the clay to mark their position, but remove them before baking the plaque.

3. Bake the plaque in a glass dish following the manufacturer's instructions. Remove the plaque from the oven, and let it cool. Glue the shells and pebbles in their imprints using super glue.

TIPS

- Microwaving polymer clay is tricky. Avoid heating the clay too long or it will crack.

- If you plan to hang your plaque, poke two holes with a pencil at the top of the plaque before baking. Tie on a raffia bow and hang.

MATERIALS

Craft paints: pink, blue, lilac, yellow, white

Wooden Alphabet and Number Blocks

Small container with lid, 5.5" x 4" x 5.5" (14 cm x 10 cm x 14 cm)

Paintbrush

Patterns: chick, heart, and star (see Patterns, pg. 40)

Pencil

Transfer paper

Silver metallic marker (see instructions on pattern)

Waterbase gloss varnish

Picture, 4.75" x 4.75" (12 cm x 12 cm)

Straightedge

Craft knife

Decoupage medium

Transparent tape

PAINTED ALPHABET BLOCKS

Decoupaged wooden alphabet and number blocks, complete with sliding lid-top box, are a thoughtful and welcomed gift for a young child. Displayed on a shelf while children are very young, stacking numbers and letters can become part of your decorating theme! Give a fresh new look to this classic learning tool by decorating the blocks to become a three-dimensional puzzle. Simply use pastel acrylic paints, a favorite picture, and decoupage medium. Note: Blocks are suitable for children three years of age and older.

INSTRUCTIONS

1. Prime all of the surfaces that will be painted with a thin coat of white paint. On 16 of the blocks, leave one side unpainted and unvarnished. The puzzle pieces will be applied to the unfinished sides.

2. In the small container, mix peach paint, using 1 part pink to 1 part yellow, and ½ part white. Mix thoroughly. Then, on each of the 32 blocks that will not be a part of the puzzle, paint one side of each block peach. Alternate between painting the solid sides and the letter or number sides of the blocks. Paint just the raised portion-the letter or number itself and the border. Paint white onto the background area of the letters and numbers. Let each color dry completely before painting the next color. Continue painting one side of each block with a new color until all blocks are completed—with the exception of the one unpainted side of the 16 blocks that will be used for the puzzle.

3. Place a sheet of transfer paper underneath the chick pattern. Trace the drawing with the pencil onto the carbon paper. Place the transfer paper face down on the lid and rub the back with a pencil. Paint the lid and let dry (see color guide on pattern). Transfer the heart pattern to the side of the box using transfer paper. Paint the side of the box, let dry, then repeat on other side of box and allow to dry. Following the same process, transfer the star pattern onto the front of the box. Paint and let dry. Repeat on the back of the box and allow to dry.

4. Apply one coat of varnish to all of the painted surfaces. Tape the picture to a cutting surface. Using a straightedge, measure and mark the picture into sixteen 1³⁄₁₆" x 1³⁄₁₆" (3.15 cm x 3.15 cm) squares. Use the straightedge and a craft knife to cut the picture along the markings.

5. Use the paintbrush to apply decoupage medium to the back of one picture piece. Adhere to the unfinished side of the block. Repeat until all of the pieces have been affixed to each of the 16 blocks. Let dry. Apply a final coat of varnish over the picture pieces. Allow everything to dry for 24 hours before putting the blocks back into the box.

TIPS

- When painting with yellow, paint only the solid sides of the blocks, not the letter or number sides. Yellow does not show up well on a white background.

- Be sure to work on a clean surface, as the paint can get scuffed or dirty before the varnish is applied.

- Find an interesting picture for the puzzle face—draw a picture, cut out a magazine or book page, or make a color copy of a favorite book illustration or photo to size. Do not use an actual photograph or any prints on heavy paper.

Photocopy at 100%

peach

white

blocks

blue

use silver metallic marker to do lettering and lines on bird

Photocopy at 143%

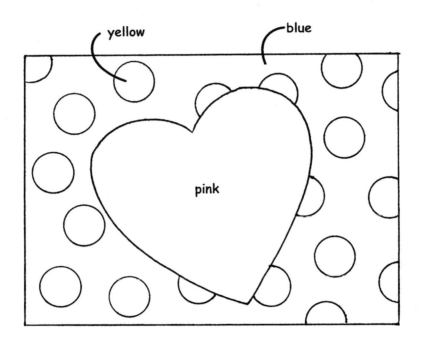

yellow

blue

pink

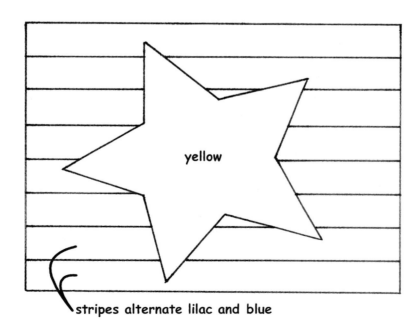

yellow

stripes alternate lilac and blue

ROOM TO GROW

CHILDREN'S BEDROOMS

When you decorate your children's rooms, you are doing more than making beautiful, colorful, and pleasant spaces—you are creating places of comfort and security. This environment, created with the colors, fabrics, wallpapers, and accessories you choose, may make a significant contribution to your children's sense of self and overall development—so make sure you have a room that pleases them, that they feel is a private haven.

Decorating and furnishing your children's rooms also can nourish their imaginations, teach important lessons, and encourage dialog. As you consider design options, include your children in the discussion. Give them a vote, which will help later with ownership and responsibility lessons. Of course, the further your children's communication skills advance, the more their individualism will surface. You will see their tastes emerge as they toss objects and ideas aside or express a preference for specific colors, patterns— even decorative objects. While preference phases are likely to come and go, it is important for parents to hear about them and discuss them with their children.

Use this chapter to find out how to decorate around the tricky transition from crib to bed, how to choose the style of furnishing that's right for you and your children, and how to decorate with pattern and color to create a flexible but fun design for your children's bedrooms. Then, share this information with them and ask questions about what they see and think. This will give you a chance to point out what you think is important for them to have in their room.

Left: A stuffed treasure and a beloved story are all within easy reach when bedtime rolls around.

Piece by Piece

When the great moment of moving your toddler from crib to bed comes, this one-time sanctuary of sleep and lullabies becomes your child's safe haven and a comfortable and cozy place for him to keep his treasures. Start your decorating scheme by considering the most costly and largest pieces in your child's room: the furniture—a bed, bureau, bedside table, bookcase or shelving, and side chairs.

The good news is today's choices are myriad: You can find beds that are small versions of antique sleigh and brass beds, and beds in clean country, ultrasleek contemporary, and fantasy shapes. Choose natural wood tones or white frames for the greatest design flexibility. Consider getting your child a bed in the Shaker style; its simple, classic lines are always in fashion and blend well with other furniture styles. For a more modern look, select fabric-covered, padded headboards that can hook onto an existing twin bed frame. Slip off the covers for easy cleaning, or replace with neutral or white fabric to create a different look in your child's bedroom.

With the bed in neutral colors, let fabrics, wall coverings, and rugs take the lead. Cover the bed with colorful patterns of animals, houses, stars, clouds, or moons. Cover cool floors with area rugs that pick up the theme. Unite disparate patterns with bed skirts, quilts, or comforters in solid hues.

Adaptability is key, so explore convertible designs—beds that grow and change as your child does. Consider choosing a crib that can convert to a toddler's bed, then a twin, and later a double. This is also a good option because you can choose good construction over a trendy color, shape, or style, and make one purchase that will last many years.

Above: Keep floors and beds natural or white to let the focus remain on the pretty patterns and one or two pieces of painted furniture. To create a delightful, engaging room, take a visual theme from a wallpaper border, such as this dressing-up vignette, and let drapes echo the theme. Choose a complementary yet simple, repetitive pattern for the rest of the wall. And don't forget a place for your children's life trophies, such as this fabric-covered bulletin board.

Above: Built-in bunk beds turn a confined space, such as the dormer side of a room, into cozy sleeping quarters for kids. You can build in a multitude of storage options: bookshelves, drawers beneath the lower bunk, and closet space. Decorate bunk bed openings with ornamental shapes to make the space even more magical for your children.

Kids' Rooms

Or, to navigate that tricky transition from crib to twin bed, use a small trundle bed that slides under a larger twin bed, to which the child can graduate eventually. The trundle will come in handy later for a slumber party guest.

Of course, safety is the first consideration when a toddler moves from a crib to a regular bed, whether a twin, double, or bunk bed. Install removable safety bars on both sides of the bed, no matter what the style. Do not allow children under the age of six to sleep on a top bunk, even with bars. For the sake of safety, make sure the spaces between the guard rails and the mattress or bars at the end of the bed are narrower than 3.5 inches (9 cm).

If your children share a room, consider getting bunk beds. Children love the coziness created by the overhead bed and the adventure of using a ladder. In general, bunk beds are fun (they make a great backbone for a massive tent), and they save on floor space. Should a conflict arise over who gets to sleep on top, transform the disagreement into an opportunity to learn to share—have them take turns.

When choosing a chest of drawers, take into account your habits and those of your child, which count in the management of your child's room. Be realistic—for example, don't buy that extra piece of furniture with six drawers if you prefer (or if it's quicker for you) to put clean clothes on shelves.

Think, too, about what will be easier and more manageable for your children to deal with when you delegate to them the responsibility of folding or storing clothes. A small bureau may work well in combination with open shelves and wall pegs for hanging things like shirts and pants. The advantage of shelves and pegs is that they can be installed at your children's height for easy access.

Set aside a place for their books, toys, stuffed animals, and special little treasures. It's important for children to know where their things are; it sets and holds the rhythm of familiarity and repetition—the qualities that give them comfort and security.

Create a wish list of the major pieces of furniture, then plan the layout of the furniture in the room, being sensitive to its relationship with the rest of the house. If you live in a condominium or apartment, place the bed on an inside wall, away from a noisy hallway. In a single-family home, consider siting the bed with a good view of a window so you can improvise a bedtime story while your child is stargazing or listening to the crickets and crows. Don't forget to take precautions, such as keeping the bed away from wall heaters and dangling shade strings. Likewise, plan for convenience; set the bed near outlets so you can install a night-light and reading light.

Finally, before you make any major furniture purchase, ask yourself these two questions:

1. **Do you plan to stay in this home for the next five years?** If not, consider these short-term, cost-effective decorating ideas: Paint your walls instead of papering; hang a swag valence over windows instead of draperies; adorn the walls with lots of family photos that go with you wherever you move; paint the floors and use area rugs instead of buying wall-to-wall carpet.

Above: Give your child a good view of a window, where they can stargaze, listen to crickets and birds, or daydream. A padded headboard provides a soft indigo backdrop that complements the whimsical wall border and bed linens.

Below: Let stuffed animals and toys reside in a special place, such as atop an unused fireplace mantel or bookshelf. If you are short on wall space, hang a shelf, rack, or ledge above the nightstand or bureau.

2. **Will this room be shared with a sibling?** For example, if you have a two-year-old and a ten-month-old, are you going to put them together in one bedroom? If so, here are some ideas for navigating sibling seas: If your kids are close in age, buy furniture that can be used by both to save money and floor space; purchase an armoire and give half to each for clothing storage; color-code wooden clothes pegs on the wall for hanging up clothes; buy one bookcase and organize the books so it's split for each. As the ten-month-old catches up with the two-year-old in tastes and needs, this system can also teach them about sharing.

Room for Creativity

An ideal technique for boosting your children's sense of comfort and pleasure is to get them involved in the design of their own room. There are no rules on how to do this, and each child's ability to communicate likes and dislikes is highly individual.

Children develop their taste buds, if you will, as early as two. For a little girl who loves ballet classes or horseback riding, choosing wallpaper with those kinds of images pleases her, feeds her imagination, keeps the interest alive, and even relaxes her when she's daydreaming in her bed. Likewise, for a little boy, seeing the things he is most interested in on his walls or floor, or on the drapery, does the same. As you're probably already attuned to your child's interests, look for ways to decorate his or her room judiciously. Keep the decorating reference to their interests meaningful by adding to decor carefully. Install wallpaper borders or artwork at the child's height, at baseboards, or at windowsill level.

Left: Your children's bedroom is as individual as they are, so be playful. If adventure and travel are what they love, cover walls, even ceilings, with framed map prints or posters.

Above: Decorate with wallpaper borders that tell a story—the cow jumping over the moon will come in handy to illustrate goodnight stories. Make sure you position the border at kid height, at the top of the chair rail or above the baseboard.

Look to colorful wallpapers, rugs, curtains, and lamps that express your children's interests, whether they are boats, trucks, or animals. These images also help you and your children talk and provide cues for little life lessons you may want to instill. You can point to the cow, or moon, or boat, and begin a spelling lesson, or make up a story with your child.

Decorating options that accomplish this include blackboard paint (which allows you to devote part of a wall to freedom of expression or a spelling lesson) and stick-on glow-in-the-dark stars. Another option is washable wallpaper that comes with loose fish or butterflies that your children can place anywhere on the wall.

Depending on how flexible you are, you can create a room that gives you freedom to change themes frequently without spending a fortune. One way you can do this is to divide the room into decorating areas. For example, you can paint or use simple patterned wallpaper on the lower levels of the walls and put the theme on the borders. You can also cover an entire wall (the lower half) with blackboard paint and introduce the border and wallpaper where it stops.

Above: Multicolored butterflies float across the wallpaper, curtains, and bedcovers to make this treetop-level room a magical place. Maintain the light, playful feeling with a painted wood floor—an easy decorating project for any mom or dad.

DESIGNING **FAMILY SPACES**

Today, design themes for our homes are more relaxed than ever before; the focus is now on comfort, practicality, and at-home pleasures. This approach has caught on in the city as well as the suburbs, and it bodes well for those raising families. With designers and architects attuned to this trend, we have more choices to help us create homes that embrace family life.

Children should be welcome everywhere in the house: You can choose fabrics, fabric protectors, floor coverings, paints, and layouts that can make your home attractive and child-friendly.

Here are ways to design the public rooms in your home with children in mind.

Entryways

With children and pets filing through this space all day long, the entry is often a difficult place to keep tidy. If you do not have the luxury of a mud room or a back door, shoes, schoolbooks, mail, and sports equipment can all end up here for a portion of the day.

Lots of little hands and muddy feet can keep you in a perpetual state of cleaning.

Above: These rounded granite countertop corners are perfect for a home with children, as are the bookshelves. Notice, too, that the kitchen chairs are covered in fabric. This gives a dressier look to the room, and if you get a washable fabric, you don't have to be concerned about spills or stains.

Above: This pup opted for sitting on the tile floor instead of the washable rag rug, but that's okay because you can vacuum his hair off the tile in a flash. When he brings in mud on his feet, a damp sponge mop will pick it right up.

Here are tips on how to make this space easy to live with:

- Choose a floor that can be washed with soap and water. Tile, stone, and linoleum can all work.
- Paint the walls and doors in the entry with a semigloss paint so you can quickly clean smudges. Keep paper towels and glass cleaner in a nearby cupboard or closet. It's a good idea to keep a mop or broom nearby too.
- Provide attractive storage options. If your children come in and take off their shoes, give them a place to put them other than the floor. Use an old trunk or a bench with storage under the seat as a shoe bin. Have another for balls and bats. Keep your mail and theirs, in separate open wooden boxes on a shelf or table, or find some interesting baskets that can become part of the design landscape. For keys that are invariably tossed here and

Above: Here is a breakfast nook that is child-friendly and easy to keep clean. The wooden tabletop—if treated with natural wax—will repel spills. The light wood chairs are easy to move and won't scratch the tile floor if they're dragged about.

Bottom Right: Who wouldn't love to have breakfast in this cheery room? The painted wood chairs and table can all be cleaned easily, and the colorful rug below catches crumbs. Don't worry about spilling on a waxed wood floor; liquid just beads, and you can pick it up with a paper towel.

there, consider a key rack or a specific basket or little box. Install a nice row of pegs to hold coats and jackets that might otherwise end up thrown over chairs. Don't forget to install pegs at your children's height!

• If the dog habitually waits for you by the front door and leaves a pile of hair and a wet bone, solve the problem by putting an extra dog bed or a dark-colored rug there. Neither the slurp nor the hair will show up. Choose a washable cover for the bed and, if you like, a washable rug.

Kitchens

More and more kitchens these days are open rooms that give whoever is cooking dinner the ability to chat with family members in other areas of the house.

If you are in the planning stage of a kitchen layout, consider creating one big, open room. Also, think about installing countertop surfaces and cupboard knobs that can be easily cleaned with a wet sponge. Look for soft,

rounded edges on counters rather than hard, square ones that could hurt when a child rounds a corner too fast and goes bump!

Another popular design element is bookshelves for storing cookbooks. Should you have them or build them, put some children's books or magazines on the lower shelves so children can browse and chat with you while you chop or knead.

If you have a growing family, with some children old enough to help in the kitchen, consider arranging storage areas so they can have access to unbreakable dishes and glasses and the family's napkins, wooden salad bowl, and tongs.

For flooring, choose a surface that's easy to clean and a pattern that won't show every speck of dirt. Stone, tile, marble, synthetic tile, and wood can all be swept clean with a damp mop. Of course, if you have very small children who will undoubtedly spill on this surface, think about how it will behave when wet. Will it turn into a slip-and-slide floor?

If you plan to put a rug in front of the sink or in the door-way, choose one with a no-skid back or put a rubber pad under it.

Consider purchasing wooden chairs instead of metal; they are less apt to hurt if a child bumps into them, they are easier to handle, and if the chair topples over or is dragged, it won't scratch the floor.

If you prefer a more sophisticated look, you can cover chairs with fabric. Choose a washable fabric that's got Velcro to keep it snug (no zippers to hurt), and treat it with a stain-resistant spray.

Of course, if you have toddlers, you must childproof the kitchen by moving all cleaning fluids and dangerous items into high cupboards. Try to put things that will interest the toddlers in the lower cupboards—pots and pans and wooden spoons; for less noise, fill low cupboards with play kitchen toys.

Above: This room has lots of childproof elements—a no-fuss wooden coffee table, a sisal rug (easy to clean; let spilled food dry, then vacuum), bookshelves the whole family can share, and washable slipcovers all around. Everyone can enjoy this pretty room.

Dens, Living Rooms, and Porches

In these busy rooms, choose furnishings, colors, and fabrics wisely. In heavy-traffic areas, choose rugs with complex patterns and deep, rich colors so the dirt won't show. Do the same for the main rugs too, especially if you have toddlers. Again, consider washable semigloss paint, washable wallpaper, or wallpaper above the touch line.

Don't worry if white is your favorite color for your couches. Just use slipcovers that are washable and tuck paper towels into the sides of every seat so you can catch a spill when it happens. If you prefer to take your chances with fancier fabrics that require professional cleaning, treat them with stain inhibitors.

With toddlers, think twice about your coffee table. Glass should not be your first choice. It may be pretty, but many a child has gotten a black eye from a glass corner. While you can put a protective cover on it, that defeats

the purpose of the table's look! So choose wood or some other material without sharp corners. Also, it's a good idea to have a drawer or two in the table for storing books or games.

Of course, the more bookshelves you have in these rooms, the better. You can store reading materials, games, and dry art supplies on them. What better way to encourage reading and family time?

In less formal rooms, like porches and sunrooms, consider furniture that's light to move about and that's bright, cheery, and welcoming. Dovetail adult items and children's, so your children really feel integrated throughout your home.

PATTERNS, COLORS, AND **TIMELESS THEMES**

Children want color, character, and life in their bedroom, so look for fabrics and wallpaper that offer style and sophistication without depending on the latest cartoon fad. Select furnishings with a white or natural finish, which makes a neutral backdrop for decorating. Paint trim and walls with light pastels, white, or neutral colors.

Reinforce a theme with **accessories.** For example, if your son loves the circus, help him collect small circus toys or stuffed animals that can be displayed on a shelf or chair top.

Create a **neutral or white backdrop** for the patterns, fabrics, and collections in your child's room. Paint the trim white and select white curtains. Look for pastel bed linens and cloth.

For little girls, anticipate the transition from a sweet, girlish style to a powerful, modern teenage scheme. Select **soft pastels** and **storybook drawings** that will give you the freedom to punch up color and accent themes with rugs, wall art, or deeper hues of complementary colors via painted furniture.

Choose themes that relate to your child's **activities and dreams**—boats, bicycles, ballet, horses, stars, flowers, circus animals, kings, and queens.

When you design around a theme, introduce **one large element** keyed to that theme rather than a host of small ones. Build a circus theme by hanging a clown mobile and covering the bed with linens that match. Create a flower theme by laying flower-shaped throw rugs, then hanging curtains keyed to their color scheme.

Remember that **adaptability** is vital when selecting your child's bedroom fashions. Pick linens and accessories that can be adapted as the child grows from toddler to elementary school student to teenager. Mix classic motifs such as toile, animals, or even chintz with stripes, gingham, or checkerboard patterns to allow a more sophisticated look later on.

DECORATING TO BUILD **SELF-ESTEEM**

Once you've made your child's room comfortable and inviting, think about ways to nourish their sense of self and to build their confidence through decor. For example, experts who study children know that as soon as they understand the concept of growing up, they begin to strive to achieve that. Make marking time and growth a design element in their rooms.

Devote a portion of a child's bedroom or playroom wall to **measuring height.** Paint or glue a yardstick on the wall and decorate it with your child's photos and special occasions that mark time.

Buy an inexpensive **bulletin board** and make a family project out of painting and decorating it. Use it as a display area for showing off school drawings, report cards, and homework with high marks.

Reserve a portion of a wall for rotating **photos that capture those special moments** you're always recording: baseball practice, taking the training wheels off a bicycle, or a first skating lesson.

Maintain a **row of photos** of each child—from birth onward—so they can see how they've grown and changed.

Start a **birthday party bulletin board** where photos and special cards hang.

If Jack's parents were planning to redesign his room, they could use this drawing to prompt a discussion on the subject. Meanwhile, here are tips for adding a bit mor fun to a child's room:

 The elevator is certainly not realistic, nor is the swing set, but maybe a faux painting on the wall behind the bed could enliven the room. It could picture a swing set or even an elevator.

The bunk bed access could be made more amusing by painting or decorating the ladder.

Another area to explore for decorating came from Boston designer Eva Dewitz, who likes to decorate television sets. Jack could work with his parents to decorate a television or the family computer. Some things that could be glued on for fun are building blocks, rods and spools, dominos, marbles, or action toys.

DECORATING TIPS
FROM THE KIDS

Jack

Jack, eight and a half years old, explained to me that this picture is of his bunk bed, and the blue object is an elevator he wished he had next to the bed. He also drew a swing set next to the bunk bed. Jack included his stuffed animals on his bed surface, added his blanket and pillow, and drew in his windows to show how his bed sits in the room.

To make a child's room more cuddly, parents could consider these options:

 Adding a down comforter to the bed and covering it with fabric that depicts cuddly things—animals, kittens, puppies, bunnies.

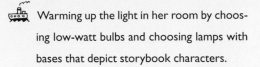 Warming up the light in her room by choosing low-watt bulbs and choosing lamps with bases that depict storybook characters.

Exploring the cozy chair idea. Does Leah want a chair for herself or one where she would sit on mom's or dad's lap for a story? Both are achievable, affordable, and could make bedtime a more pleasant experience. Perhaps a beanbag chair with a big, fluffy throw would suffice. If space is tight, a reading pillow—the kind that hugs your sides—would do the trick. Add a few velcro tabs, then apply a row of little stuffed animals onto each arm of the pillow!

Leah

When Leah was asked what she wished she had in her room, she drew two things: a girl in a cozy chair and her sister, Anna, in bed. She really loves sharing a room with her sister. To four-year-olds, being cuddly and secure takes the lead over design!

AT SAMANTHA'S HOUSE

Samantha's mom, Debbie, promised herself that when she became a mom, she would never have "no touch" and "don't go there" zones in her home. It is much more important to her that Samantha enjoys their home.

It is obvious when you step into the home she shares with her daughter and husband that Debbie accomplished her goal. Each public room has comfortable seating and tasteful furnishings, but nothing feels contrived or "set up." Rather, there are nice antiques and rows of family photographs that express a cozy intimacy. The design attitude seems to say, "Sit here. Get comfy. Enjoy the view." That attitude continues in Samantha's little suite, which includes a bedroom, sitting room, and bath.

Debbie felt it was important for Samantha's growth and sense of self to have a place where she was comfortable and that she knew was hers. She started off in the room in her crib, and by the time she was two, she was in a double bed. When she is ill or feeling insecure, her mom soothes her in her own space and sometimes even sleeps next to her.

In anticipation of Samantha's arrival (her parents knew the baby was a girl), her mom and Mark, her dad, purchased the bed and crib and decided to decorate with a pink floral wallpaper. This caused some disagreement. Debbie wanted a yellow room, and Mark wanted a very feminine room with wallpaper.

"I wanted it to look like retro '50s, and he wanted it to be pink!" says Debbie. But Mark's interest in his new baby's room melted her heart, and the floral paper went up.

collection needed a home. At one point, a dollhouse was discussed, but Samantha's preference for inflatable chairs seemed like a nice decorating idea and suited her interests.

Some thoughtful design elements are worth noting in these rooms. For example, Samantha's bed is positioned in a corner between two big windows with seats instead of against an empty wall. She can climb into bed, look at the sky and mature trees to the left and right, and daydream. Curtains frame the window, and the valance punctuates the wonderful height.

Samantha is an avid dancer and quite concerned with her form—hence the mirror on a light wood stand at the foot of the bed. Another personal touch is the big chair next to the bed where the stuffed animals live. They all have names, and their proximity makes it convenient for Sam to grab one to join her for a nap or a chat. The chair's design and neutral color highlight the colorful pile of stuffed animals.

Nothing in here is fancy or untouchable. Samantha's parents have given her

They chose a simple, Shaker-style bed and, over time, added pertinent details as Samantha's interests developed. For example, the mirror at the foot of the bed lets her check her dance form. Likewise, the growing stuffed animal

the freedom to enjoy and organize the room to suit herself.

At one point, the sitting room was going to be a playroom, but Samantha really wanted it to be a place where she could sit and read. The lesson here is that once you begin a dialog with your children about their space, you can make discoveries that surprise and please you. Beyond that, you can work with your children to make a room a place they will use fully.

Samantha's sitting room is more like an adult's than a child's—except for two brightly colored inflatable chairs, where she reads and draws, and her doll collection (in the antique armoire). Another small doll collection sits on a wall shelf opposite the armoire, and a simple, low bookshelf is nearby.

That she loves the chairs is terrific, and that they are vinyl and easy to clean with a damp sponge is a benefit as well. Think about this kind of furniture for your children's spaces. It's durable, has no springs to wear out, and, having no fabric to stain, is easy to maintain.

For extra storage space in your child's room, consider using an armoire for toys, books, clothes, or all three. The lower portion of Samantha's armoire holds towels and bathing suits. The little wall shelf is an example of a storage approach that adds color and texture to a room. Instead of dolls, put photos, a Beanie Babies collection, or even more books. You can purchase raw wood shelves and paint them or cover them with wallpaper.

A real life design success, Samantha's room is her sanctuary.

MATERIALS

Plush felt, 4 sheets, 18" x 22.5" (46 cm x 57 cm), 1 dark heather brown, 2 white, 1 light heather or tan

2 pillows, 16" (41 cm) square

Sticky-backed felt, 9" x 12" (23 cm x 30 cm), red, white, black

Six strand embroidery floss, 8.75 yd. (8 m), 1 black, 1 red

Polyester stuffing, 16 oz bag

Patterns (see pg. 70)

Sewing machine and thread

Hand-sewing needle

Embroidery needle

Scissors

Ruler

Light colored pencil (white or yellow)

CRAFTING WITH KIDS

PUPPY PILLOW TRIO

These three imaginative pillows brighten up a puppy-inspired decorating theme in a child's room. Easy patterns and simple shapes mean you can sew them in no time. And the appliqués are cut from sticky-back felt! The dog house and bone-shaped pillows are the perfect complement to the adorable black-and-white pup on the third pillow. You can easily follow the same steps using patterns you create to coordinate with the theme of your child's room.

INSTRUCTIONS

Dog bone pillow

1. Tape dog bone pattern piece 1 to pattern piece 2 as indicated on the patterns. Place the pattern on the folded white plush. Trace the pattern and cut out. This will yield two bones. Place the two pieces with right sides together (plush to plush), and sew from dot to dot, leaving an opening to stuff. Turn bone right side out, and stuff with polyester filling until plump. Slipstitch the remaining seam closed.

Doghouse pillow

1. Mark the doghouse pillow pattern. On the wrong side of the dark brown plush draw a 17" x 12" (43 cm x 30 cm) rectangle, using the light colored pencil so that the lines are clearly visible. On a long side, measure over 8.5" (22 cm), and mark the center with a notch. Repeat, making an identical rectangle on a second sheet of dark brown plush. Cut out each rectangle.

2. On the wrong side of the remaining piece of felt, draw two triangles that each measure 15" x 15" x 23" (38 cm x 38 cm x 58 cm). On the longest side, measure over 11.5" (29 cm), and mark the center with a notch. Cut out each triangle. Matching notches, sew each triangle to a rectangle using a .5" (1 cm) seam allowance.

3. With right sides together, sew the front of the doghouse to the back of the doghouse, leaving a 6" (15 cm) opening along the bottom edge. Turn the pillow right side out and stuff the triangle (the roof) with poly-fil. Insert a pillow form into the rectangle section and slip stitch the remaining seam closed. Where the triangle meets the rectangle, tie three quilter's tacks with the red embroidery floss. Trace the door patterns onto the red and the black felt. Trace the letters onto the white felt. Referring to the photograph for placement, peel back the paper, and place the door and the lettering on the pillow.

Puppy pillow

1. Cut out two 17" x 17" (43 cm x 43 cm) squares from the tan plush. With right sides together, sew along all edges, leaving a 6" (15 cm) opening along one side. Turn right side out and stuff the pillow with a pillow form. Slip stitch the remaining seam closed.

2. Trace the dog patterns onto the red, black, and white felt. Cut out the white dog. Peel the paper from the back of the felt, and place the dog in the center of the pillow. Cut out the red dog collar. Peel paper from the back of the felt, and place it around the dog's neck. Cut out the black eyes, nose, and two spots. Peel paper from the back of the felt, and place all the pieces as indicated by the illustration. Outline the entire dog by hand-sewing a blanket stitch with black embroidery thread.

TIPS

- Design a custom pillow that looks just like your pup. Use a favorite photograph as the basis for your pattern.

- Short Cuts: For a no-sew variation on these adorable pillows, glue felt shapes to ready made pillows. Or, outline pattern pieces on plain cotton pillow covers and color with textiles paints or crayons. Follow product instructions for setting colors.

PUPPY PILLOW TRIO PATTERNS

Photocopy at 167%

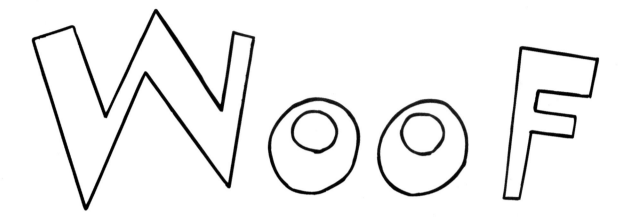

Photocopy at 200%

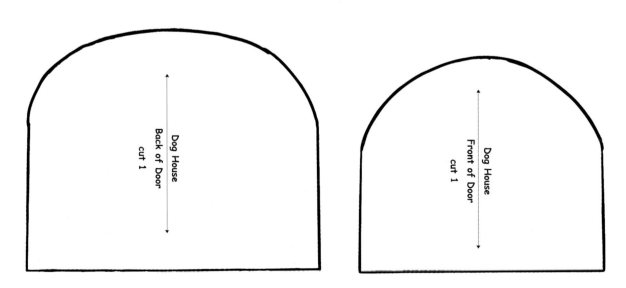

Photocopy at 333%

Puppy Pillow
Eyes
cut 1

Puppy Pillow
Nose
cut 1

Puppy Pillow
Spot
cut 1

Puppy Pillow
Tail
cut 1

Puppy Pillow
Collar
cut 1

Puppy Pillow
Placement Guide
Do Not Cut

Puppy Pillow
Dog Body cut 1

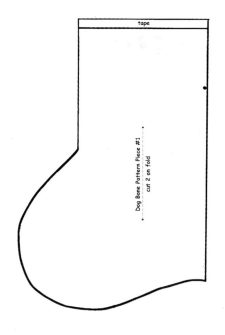

tape

Dog Bone Pattern Piece #1
cut 2 on fold

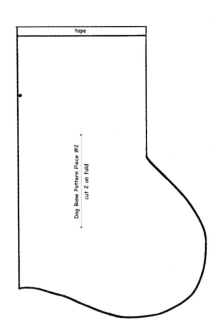

tape

Dog Bone Pattern Piece #2
cut 2 on fold

MATERIALS

Several Foam sheets, 2mm,
9" × 12" (23 cm x 30 cm),
in various colors

Dimensional fabric and
craft paint, in various colors

Broad point black
permanent marker

Scallop edge scissors

Pinking scissors

Regular edge scissors

Round hole punch

Opaque broad point pen, white

Blow dryer

Pen or pencil

SEASONAL PICTURE FRAMES

These picture frames are   colorful foam sheets,
an inexpensive medium that's easy to work with. Make several seasonal frames to decorate a wall of your child's room
with a progression of photos chronicling his growth over the
course of a year. Kids love to see how little they used to be.

INSTRUCTIONS

Autumn Frame

1. Cut out shapes. (See patterns, page 74). With a pen or pencil, trace the pattern pieces onto the color foam sheets. Cut out the leaf shapes using pinking, regular, and scallop edge scissors.

2. Decorate shapes: Paint "veins" on the leaves with dimensional paint to match the color of the leaf. Set aside and let dry for 1 to 2 hours. Or, use a blow-dryer on a low setting to speed up the drying time.

3. Make the background. Using the scallop scissors, trim along the outside edges of all 4 sides of background color foam. Then, make dots all over the sheet with white dimensional paint. Let dry.

4. Attach photo to frame: Affix a photo to the center of the tan foam sheet by placing a small amount of tacky glue on the photo's edges. Arrange the leaves around the photo and glue in place.

SEASONAL PICTURE FRAMES PATTERNS

Photocopy at 182%

Photocopy at 250%

Double Pumpkin

Photocopy at 182%

eyes/buttons

nose

mitten

mitten

scarf

arm

branches

ROOM TO RETREAT

STUDIES AND STORAGE

Children need a retreat in the home, same as you do. Unless space is abundant, children often sleep, study, play, and store personal items in their bedrooms. This multipurpose approach is certainly doable, but to create an attractive, organized, child-friendly space with all these functions takes planning and research. Before making any purchase, think about how to make the room's design work hard. Your child should want to spend time in the room, enjoy it, and be comfortable doing homework and projects there.

For this book, I interviewed and observed children ages three to nine and was impressed with how much each loved his or her room and had definite ideas about what he or she liked and needed. While a three-year-old can not be interviewed per se, I spent time in many kids' rooms and noticed how they loved being there. From sunny rooms with great treetop views of the neighborhood, to rooms with plenty of floor space on which to spread games and toys, the best designs are rooms that can grow with the children.

This chapter includes children's bedrooms that accommodate various activities. It also describes situations where study areas are merged with family spaces. The latter examples illustrate how, if a bedroom is too small for a desk or storage, these functions can be successfully introduced in common areas. Whether you have to split your child's activities between rooms or not, it's worth the effort to create a retreat that gives them space—quiet space to read, think, imagine, and study.

Storage by Design

Storage space is critical to making bedrooms work and should not be overlooked in the plans for children's rooms, no matter what their age. Plan to devote a corner or part of a wall to book storage. In fact, the more places your child can access reading material, the better. Consider installing a single shelf right near the bed so your child can choose the evening's storybook and stuffed animal easily.

If your children's rooms are big enough for them to play in, consider having carpeting or a throw rug on one side and linoleum on the other—a wet and dry side. Kids can learn to bring out their paints on the wet side, and you don't have to warn them to be careful so often.

Toys, drawing materials, and prized homework all need an easily accessible storage place. Toys can go into all kinds of imaginative containers that can coordinate with the room's palette. For example, buy wicker laundry baskets and spray-paint them. Teach your children colors and names by painting them different colors and making signs for what's inside; use one for trucks, another for balls, etc.

Drawing materials can be kept in cardboard boxes that the children decorate to match the room. Boxes can be painted or accented with fabric swatches that match the curtains or borders you've chosen. This kind of activity stimulates creativity and gives children a sense of ownership and orderliness.

Above: Here is a creative, attractive way to make storage a major design component in your child's room. Open shelves with varying depths allow a mix of objects to be stored and offer opportunities to segregate and organize items. Cabinets keep frequently used toys in reach and can hold awkwardly shaped items.

Above: Another way to coordinate storage areas and save money is to purchase sturdy wooden furniture from a secondhand store or flea market and hand-paint it to match the theme of the room. Here, a desk and storage bin have been painted with a nature theme.

Storage as a Design Element

One thing every parent soon realizes is that there can never be too much storage space. With each growth phase come more books, drawing tools, toys, sports equipment, clothes, videos, CDs, and more. These things spill into the rest of the house if storage in the bedroom is inadequate. With a little creative planning, you can find storage solutions that not only are practical but also become a major design element in your child's room.

If budget allows, consider building in bookshelves and anchoring them with storage cabinets. The more space devoted to them, the better items can be stored and displayed. Two shelves assigned to colorful stuffed animals become a design element. Store items your children play with frequently on the lower shelves and cabinets. The cabinets can be used for their favorite items, and because they have doors that close, mess is not an issue. This system works well for children of all ages. Young children, in particular, like to go into their own cubbyholes for their toys.

Another option, if your child will remain in this room for several years or if space is limited, is to work with a carpenter to custom-design a structure that accommodates storage and a work surface. A simple, clean-lined design in wood allows you to easily change the room's palette to accommodate the next child, girl or boy, and remains in style for several years.

If both space and budget are limited, consider having a single custom-built piece that, by it's design, gives your child's room a dash of color and whimsy. It may function at first as a toy and book storage area;

Above: Utilize wasted space by building a window seat with storage underneath. Here, adding a Humpty Dumpty hat rack introduces color and texture to a wall while adding more practical storage.

Opposite: If you have the space to put a window seat along a wall, obtain even more storage by putting drawers beneath. In this room, the window seat is wide enough for a few children to sit and read, with easy access to books and toys below.

later, when your child is older, it may be better suited for clothes or sports items.

See whether or not the windows can accommodate a window seat. This is a great way to utilize what could be wasted space and to offer your child a pleasant place to read or play—with storage beneath. A window seat can be custom built, or you can improvise with a big, flat-topped trunk or toy chest. If the trunk needs sprucing up, tackle the painting project together with your child.

Another terrific storage solution is an armoire. Depending on your preference, choose an antique, a family heirloom or hand-me-down, one that's unfinished (ready to paint), or a flea market find. The latter two can be painted to match the room, or have some fun and paint on a pattern, texture, or outdoor scenes. A carpenter can add shelves, if necessary, and leave the bottom like an open bin for even more storage.

Personalizing the Study Zone

Children's study areas, perhaps more than any other area in their rooms, reflect who they are, what their interests are, and who they are becoming. They come here for privacy, inspiration, reflection, and creativity. When it's time to decide where to put the desk—in front of a window or tucked into a corner—ask them where they would like to be. Plan the study area with your son or daughter, with you guiding the discussion and inviting feedback. The goal is to create a place to which your child feels connected and that you think works functionally and visually.

Where does planning begin? A good first step, after determining where the desk will go, is to ask your children for decoration preferences. Cue them to help. Your son, for example, may have tucked away his collection of dinosaurs but still likes looking at them. Suggest a shelf for them. The bright colors and varied shapes will provide texture and color in the space.

Other items that can enhance a study area are photos of family and friends, trophies, and framed school papers they are proud of. To ensure the area remains visually pleasing, provide the tools needed to keep these items organized. Here are some examples:

- Install bulletin boards—one for special school papers, another for drawings, and another for special dates like sporting events and recitals.
- Go to a flea market and look for unusual boxes in paper or wood, then create a collage on a shelf or the floor. If your daughter loves hats, for example, search for old hatboxes and create a windowsill display/storage area.
- Purchase new or old tin containers—the more variety in shape and size, the better. If they need to be freshened with paint, make this a joint decorating project with your child. Paint on letters that describe what will be stored inside, or just have fun and make bright, energizing design elements.
- Use curtains that have little pockets sewn onto them for storing light items like tiny toys, marbles, or even photos. Try making them yourself, using different materials for the pockets. Trim with ribbon, denim, or whatever suits your fancy.

Above and Opposite: These rooms offer well-lit study space and lots of places to personalize and tuck away treasures—desk, bookshelves, and a high shelf on the wall for display.

Above: Here is a great way to combine functions in a room. A floor-to-ceiling bookshelf acts as a room divider separating the study zone from the play area. Homework and drawings on the walls personalize the room.

- Purchase a variety of cardboard boxes and paint them with your child, or cover them in fabric that matches the room. Cut off the top closures and line the boxes up on the floor or a bookshelf.

- Find a three-panel privacy screen or room divider, cover it in fabric that complements the room, and stitch on a dozen pockets in different colors and sizes. Mix and match fabrics and patterns to make this even more visually appealing.

- If wicker is compatible with the room design, purchase a wicker hamper for toy storage. Spray-paint it to match the room, and line it with fabric that matches the window treatments.

- For big, awkward items, consider introducing a trunk for storage.

- Stackable plastic crates make a good, inexpensive storage solution. Remember not to put heavy, sharp objects in these, and don't stack them too high, just in case they tip over.

- If space is very tight and the window has an unattractive view, look into having a 2- or 3-foot-high (.6 m or .9 m) shelf made that sits on the windowsill and mimics panes. Do not do this, however, if the window functions as a fire escape.

Above: Take an inventory of your child's personal items and decide what you need to accommodate. In this room, the bunk bed had a desk and storage built in, but more freestanding storage was needed to accommodate games.

Left: If you're handy with a saw, cut plywood in an interesting shape to enclose your child's bed, then paint it to match a theme. For more storage, replicate the shape in smaller versions and close it with a roof.

KIDS' STORAGE IN **FAMILY LIVING SPACES**

Consider locating children's books and toys in family living space—try cabinets, bookshelves, even fireplace mantels. Thus, when you are in the kitchen or family room, you can converse with your children while they play or color. This is a wonderful way to show that children are on board, and it makes them feel as important as you in the home.

Take the same approach in bathrooms. Keep children's towels, soaps, and bath toys in lower cabinets or shelves so they can help prepare for their bath. Choose a small hamper for them to throw their own towels and dirty clothes into; it's a nice training ground for being orderly and responsible.

If you have pets your children can safely feed, consider storing the pet food in a place the children can access. Feeding pets gives kids a sense of ownership. Your child can paint or color a food holder for your pet hamster, bunny, or fish.

Set aside cabinet space in the living room or family room for children's toys. Children can go into their own cupboards and play while Mom or Dad is within range to watch them and chat.

Do you cook a lot? Put baskets of toys in lower kitchen cupboards. The children can play on the floor nearby while you work. Likewise, devote a low shelf in the kitchen or living room to toys or dry snacks so your child feels part of the family scene.

SOLVING THE **NO-CLOSETS** PROBLEM

The list of things you have to store for your children can send you reeling! Instead of panicking or threatening to throw out everything without a home, turn the tables and have a little fun. Here are some imaginative storage solutions to consider if you have a playroom but not enough closets.

Save old milk cartons, shipping cartons, and juice bottles. When they dry out, paint them and fill them with marbles, crayons, paintbrushes, rulers, and scissors.

Scour flea markets for old wooden boxes, or take apart an old desk and use the drawers as storage space; chances are they'll stack. Have the handyman of the house attach wheels to the boxes and drawers. Attach string or ribbon to the knobs and your children can transport drawers full of toys to the family room and back to their rooms in a flash. Decorate all of these with paint, fabric, or both.

Purchase a set of brightly colored bed sheets, feed a wire through the sewn ends, and attach the wire at ceiling height to two nails, one on each end. Or, purchase fabric and iron-on hems, and attach the same way to the wall. This wall of fabric will hide lots of toys.

Purchase a card table or two and cover with fabric; store toys and games underneath.

COMPUTER PLACEMENT AND STORAGE

It's best to put your child's computer in a public area of the home, according to *Boston Globe* parenting columnist and author Barbara Meltz, who researches children's computer usage *(Put Yourself in Their Shoes, Understanding How Your Children See the World)*. She urges parents to be involved in their children's computer activities. Show them that the computer is a useful appliance, not a form of entertainment. Monitoring is difficult if the computer is in the child's room, but if there is no choice, keep the modem in view so you can monitor Internet use.

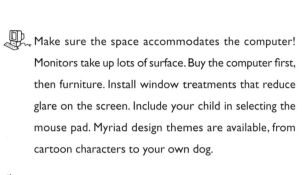 Make sure the space accommodates the computer! Monitors take up lots of surface. Buy the computer first, then furniture. Install window treatments that reduce glare on the screen. Include your child in selecting the mouse pad. Myriad design themes are available, from cartoon characters to your own dog.

A chair that swivels and moves up and down is handy— the swivel for turning from the computer to another work surface, the height adjustment when children share the space.

Accent the desk with your child's prized collections. This work space should be both comfortable and inspiring.

Spend time with your child choosing a screen saver. Sound effects and action can enliven the space but may send the wrong message.

Choose sturdy desktop storage bins for supplies. Vary the sizes, shapes, and colors for visual interest.

Select a lamp that serves all the tasks undertaken at the desktop. Three-way bulbs offer both general and task-specific lighting. Floor lamps with adjustable necks illuminate both reading chairs and the computer table.

For instant neatness, house the computer in an armoire. New models are designed with computers in mind and offer storage as well. Antique armoires can be reworked for this purpose.

BATHROOM **TILES**

Today, bathrooms are given more and more design attention. If you step into a tile showroom these days, you will find a plethora of tiles specifically designed for children's baths and featuring themes from romping bears to Noah's ark. If you are considering devoting a bathroom in your home to a child or children, keep in mind these design guidelines and suggestions for tile use.

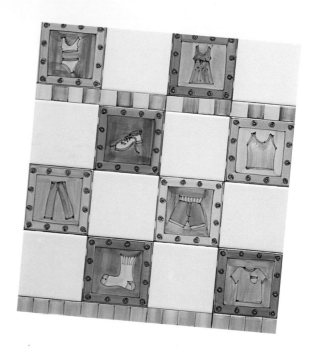

 Consider using tile with geometric patterns or generic themes like the beach or animals if the bathroom will be shared by boys and girls.

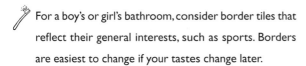 For a boy's or girl's bathroom, consider border tiles that reflect their general interests, such as sports. Borders are easiest to change if your tastes change later.

Be careful not to choose trendy tile themes that may go out of style quickly.

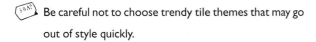

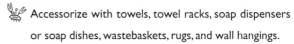 Trail decorative tiles around a window frame, or make patterns on the floor. You can create interesting, amusing patterns that direct your child's attention to the sink, tub, shower, or a great view outside.

Accessorize with towels, towel racks, soap dispensers or soap dishes, wastebaskets, rugs, and wall hangings.

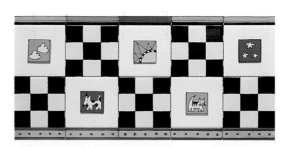

Anna's second drawing depicts a current favorite item in her room, her calendar. This can cue a numbers and time theme in which to redecorate.

- ☼ Allow Anna to draw an oversized monthly calendar on a roll of paper installed at her height on the wall.

- 🐝 Cut out felt numbers, punch holes on the tops, string ribbon through, and hang with tiny nails or hooks across a wall.

- ✈ Zone the room by season. Paper each wall with an appropriate visual. Accessorize with stuffed animals that live in cold and warm weather, curtains with a sky or cloud pattern, or a miniature collection of sleighs on a shelf. Anna could draw snowflakes and hang them in the winter windows, and draw flowers for spring windows.

Anna

Anna's computer is in the family room. Asked if she could change anything in her bedroom, she drew a desk with a computer. Notice the attention to detail—two vases of flowers, a colored monitor, and desk drawer details. This six-year-old has a design vision!

However, Anna shares the computer with several siblings. Perhaps her parents can add a fresh-picked flower in a bud vase or a little plant that can be taken off the work surface for watering. It seems being pretty matters to Anna! Another way to personalize the computer area is to have photos of family members on a bulletin board nearby to generate a sense of community.

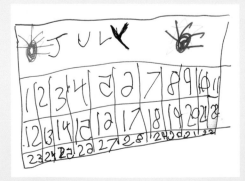

Miles

I think Miles really drew his life wish rather than what he wanted in his room. When I sat with him weeks before he drew this, he told me that he wished for a secret kitchen over his bedroom. That way, whenever he wanted a snack, he could climb into his secret kitchen and get whatever he wanted.

Actually, having a little box in his room, perhaps decorated with his drawings of food, could be a cute storage area for healthy snacks. It could hold a few small bags. That way, when he is playing by himself or with a friend, he can go to his own cupboard! An empty oatmeal box could become an art project to then store animal crackers or pretzels.

Miles is five and crazy about dogs. When I asked him what he wished he had in his room, he drew a dog at his computer! In reality, his computer is in his den, surrounded with plastic prehistoric animals.

The fact is, the timing is not right for Miles to have a dog—but he is taken with them. Perhaps a way to encourage his healthy appreciation of dogs is to bring a modest dog design theme into his room.

- Place a scatter rug with a big dog face at his bedside.

- Line a wall with a row of photos or drawings of his favorite dogs in the neighborhood.

- Find a dog clock that barks a different bark to mark each hour. Each hour has the face of a different dog. Alternatively, someone who is handy could make a clock with a dog's face.

AT MILES'S HOUSE

When Suzi and Steve bought a two-bedroom city condominium, they wanted to maximize their limited space and create a child-friendly, stimulating home for their son. One of the first things they decided to do was give Miles the bigger of the two bedrooms, the one with a pleasant bay window with city views. The goal was to give him a room where he could play, store lots of toys, and have a friend sleep over. Likewise, the second full bath was assigned to Miles and decorated for him as well. Responsibility for this chunk of real estate gives him a clear message that he is both important and accountable for keeping his things in order.

The large bedroom accommodates big, awkward items like a drum set and easel. If your home has similar space limitations, consider giving your child or children the larger bedrooms, assuming this makes sense given the overall layout. Suzi and Steve could have put Miles in a smaller room or even the den, which is in another wing. Sensibly, however, they realized that while he could bang his drums all he wanted there, storage would be inadequate. Containing bedrooms in the back wing and placing the living room, dining room, kitchen, and den in the front provide everyone with space for privacy and quiet when needed.

The fact is, Miles can play the drums in his room without bothering his parents in the front wing. If he challenges Steve to a game of chess, they can play in the living room or dining room.

Miles's board games, dinosaur collection, and computer programs are neatly arranged in the den. This room is nicely divided for Miles's games and his parents' books and equipment. He shares the computer with his dad, so Steve's work notes may be anchored by a convenient dinosaur!

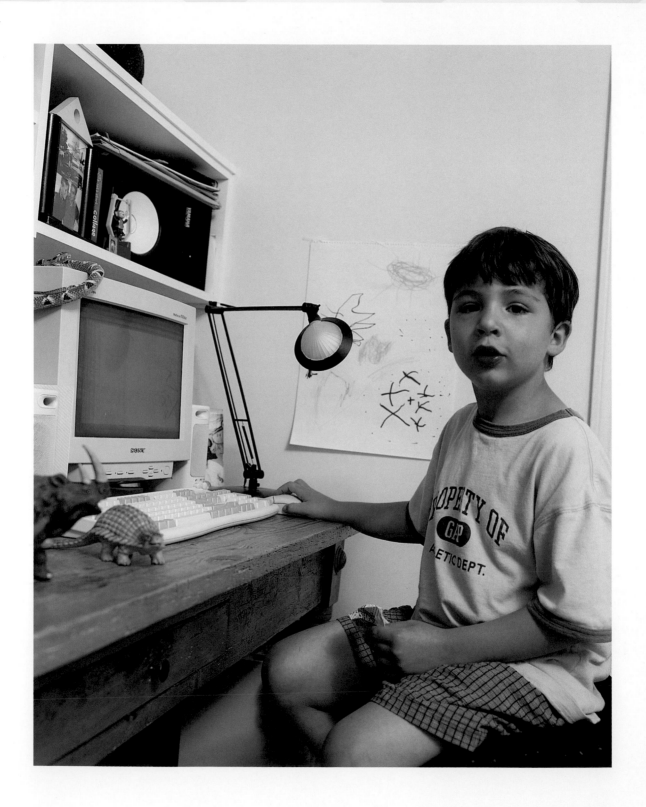

Kids' Rooms

Another inclusive gesture Suzi made was to purposefully store things at Miles's level, within easy reach. "Everything should be easy for Miles to find—that way he doesn't have to constantly ask me where things are. Also, this lets him feel independent because he has access to these things—he has the sense that the house is available to him—except when it comes to food!" his mom says.

Shelves, bookcases, and storage drawers in Miles's closet all come in handy, and what goes where is up to him. Suzi observes, "It's his agenda, his choices. He feels he can go deep with that, on his own terms. And for him, as an only child, it works—his imagination becomes easily engaged."

She and Miles also spend time together in the kitchen. He enjoys working by her side, using measuring cups and stirring pots. Implements he uses are stored within his reach.

"We're in 1,500 square feet of space, and we've made it so he has choices on where to be—the den, his bedroom, the dining room—and with what—his books, cards, marbles, Beanie Babies. He doesn't need permission to do these things, and it gives him a sense of purpose and accomplishment. It has afforded him an 'I can do' attitude and lets him know he does not need someone with him all the time," she adds.

MATERIALS

Opaque broad point pens:
red, blue, green, yellow,
white, and black

Two clear acrylic tool boxes
or organizer carry-alls

Crafter's glue
(make sure it adheres to plastic)

FUNKY TOOL BOX

Special boxes for special "tools" help keep things neat, and the boxes themselves can be lively additions to a child's space. Transform an ordinary tool box into a fun, personalized carry-all with easy to use paint markers. Kids of all ages can get involved—simply draw decorations on the clear box and use it to hold crafts, toys, school supplies, even as a lunch box. Paint marker ink takes a minute to dry, but once it does, it's permanent. This is a project for everyone in the family! Materials make two tool boxes.

INSTRUCTIONS

1. Plan your design. Make stencils by tracing the clipart below.

2. Shake and start markers according to package directions.

3. Beginning at the bottom of the box, place the stencils and trace around them, and color in the outlines. Or, if you are comfortable, decorate with free-hand shapes, numbers, and letters. To avoid smudges, allow each section to dry for one minute before you continue.

4. With crafters' glue apply buttons, small plastic trinkets, foam cutouts, feathers, or other found objects for a 3-D design. (Avoid using glitter—though fun and decorative, it tends to fall off. You'll be sweeping up glitter for months!)

5. The paint will dry in one minute. See manufacturer's instructions for glue drying time. Use your imagination and have fun.

TIP

Draw your words and pictures on plain white paper and tape them underneath the area you want to decorate. Then trace the designs with the color markers.

Photocopy at varying sizes

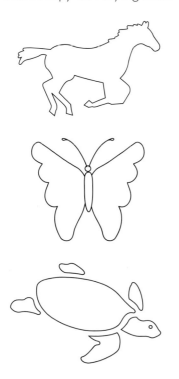
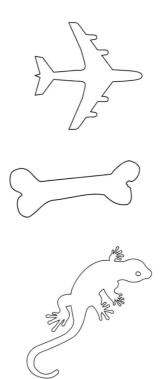

MATERIALS

Cork sheet 24" x 48"
(61 cm x 122 cm)

Ruler

Craft knife

White craft glue

Small paint brush

Acrylic paints, green
and dark green

Scissors

Modeling clay: black, red, turquoise,
white, yellow, and violet

Waxed paper for work surface

Clay blade or single edge
razor blade

Glass baking dish

Thumb tacks

FUN BUG TACKS AND
PAINTED CORKBOARD

Use your imagination to create fantasy clay bug thumbtacks
that live on a painted grass cork sheet. Get kids involved in
this project and have fun! The board will provide a special spot
for your child's choice of art projects, school notices, or special photos to display.

INSTRUCTIONS

1. Roll out and flatten the sheet of cork. Measure, mark and cut three 6" x 24" (15 cm x 61 cm) strips of cork. Glue the 3 strips one on top of the other with white craft glue to create a triple thickness of the cork. Lay flat and let the glue dry.

2. Roughly sketch simple, grass shapes along the length of the cork. Paint them in dark green, and let dry. Sketch some more simple, grass shapes along the length of the cork, overlapping the darker, green shapes. Paint them in green, and allow to dry.

3. Create bug bodies from basic shapes. Roll the clay into balls of various colors and sizes from .25" (.5 cm) round to 1" (3 cm) round. Slice the balls in half with the razor blade. Make oval shapes and cut in half lengthwise. Roll out some flat sheets and cut wing shapes, small squares, and triangles with the craft knife. Dots can be made by rolling very small balls, and then flattening them out with your finger. Combine shapes to make the bugs. Make sure all colors and shapes are pressed together well before baking. Use a pencil point to make indentations for eyes.

4. Bake the modeling clay bugs according to package directions in a glass baking dish.

5. Glue thumb tacks to the backs of the bugs. Allow glue to dry. Hang the bulletin board to your wall using small nails or double sided tape.

TIPS

• Use a few heavy books to flatten the cork as the glue dries.

• Make extra bugs, and glue magnets on the backs for the refrigerator.

• Short Cut: Buy a decorated bulletin board so you can use your limited craft time on creature creation.

ROOM TO ROAM

PLAY AREAS INSIDE AND OUT

O<small>FTEN, WHEN FAMILIES ARE GROWING</small> and there is a mix of toddlers and young children in the home, toys, games, books, and art projects begin to spill into all rooms of the house. A dedicated playroom, if space permits, can not only help you keep things in check but also offer your children a place to play among themselves, or with friends in a room that totally serves their interests.

A playroom is not meant to segregate the children from family life; rather, it is a little piece of the home that caters to their needs, a place where they can play in a carefree setting. A playroom is a great place for children to gather after school or in inclement weather, and the perfect locale for completing an art project. When the children are old enough to comprehend their ownership of the room, they can begin to learn lessons in organization and how to keep the room tidy.

Likewise, outdoor play space is a wonderful way to get your children fresh air, sunshine, and exercise. It can teach them about nature and the outdoors, and keep them under your watchful eye.

This chapter is meant to inspire you on the possibilities of indoor and outdoor play spaces by illustrating a variety of solutions and design elements and showing you how to achieve them. These playrooms include inside rooms as well as backyard tree houses.

As you browse these pages, note how you might adapt a design, layout, and furnishing solutions to suit your family's needs. Creating playrooms can turn out to be family building or painting projects, depending on your interests, talents, and budget.

Left: Locate an indoor playroom near an outdoor play area, if possible. These railings are painted in bright, appealing colors to lead the way to fun. The rugs are the perfect dark gray to handle lots of traffic. Furnishings are simple and functional—a game table and soft beanbag chairs. An inviting little coat- and hatrack is beside the door.

Creative Solutions for Indoor Play Spaces

Where Do You Put a Playroom?

Ideally, a playroom is located within the range of adult supervision or earshot. Listening to the way your children play can teach you a lot about their personality and communication skills. If there is an emergency or a disagreement in which you need to intervene, being steps away helps. Beyond that, windows that let in the daylight and fresh air make the playroom—or any room—a pleasant place to be.

If space allows, segregate the noisier musical instruments from the playroom. In fact, if your children are all interested in music, consider turning a portion of your basement into a music room. Miles, a young boy featured in chapter three, keeps his drum set in his bedroom, which is located down the hall from the kitchen and den. His city condominium doesn't have a playroom, but when he plays his drums, his parents can be in the living room and still hear one another.

How Do You Organize It?

A playroom can house just about anything your children play with. Help them maximize its use by creating a layout that divides the room into compartments.

For example, split the room into a wet side and dry side. The wet side can hold paints, markers, clay, bubbles—anything that can spill or mark and stain the surroundings.

On the dry side, store the following:

- puzzles
- board games
- sports equipment
- dolls
- books
- television

- building blocks
- videotapes
- toys for playing make-believe including:
     kitchen setup
     doctor's bag,
     fireman's outfit

Above: What could be more appropriate for the wet side of a room than a water theme? And who says the chairs have to match? Chairs in different styles and colors make this room more fun. Notice the sea creatures painted on them—a nice touch to carry the overall theme.

Opposite: Your children will likely love the same rooms you do! Windows that let in fresh air and sunshine are highly desirable; this room illustrates the point perfectly. Notice also the flooring—big, multicolored rubber puzzle pieces—great for little kids, who take the occasional spill. The room offers plenty of pint-sized seating and activities.

If possible, color code shelves and the containers that they house: a blue sticker on the "puzzle shelf" and matching stickers on the puzzle boxes can make clean up easy and fun for kids and their friends.

A bulletin board is a handy feature. Post your children's parties, sporting events, school outings, and birthdays of friends and teachers in view. Help the kids personalize the board and decorate it together.

Another good family project is making a crafts box for the playroom. Fill it with pipe cleaners, colorful yarn, buttons, glitter, and stickers for imaginative play.

If the room has no closet, it's a good idea to store a roll of paper towels—perhaps on a dispenser—near the paints and markers, and a dustpan tucked under a shelf or bookshelf.

Floors

Should you decide to divide the room into wet and dry sides, consider using linoleum tiles or vinyl that comes in sheets for the whole room. Then, for the dry side, or a portion thereof, add an area rug, which allows children to do puzzles or construct toy train tracks on a level, quiet surface.

Make the floor a major design element by choosing bright, colorful linoleum tiles and creating an interesting pattern or map of the room's specific areas. For example, designate yellow as the main color and use red tiles to lead to the paint and easel section, blue tiles to the television and video area, and green to the bookshelves. The colored tiles act like little roadways that stop at each area. Explore the possibility of having linoleum tiles custom-cut to interesting shapes. Center the wet area with a multicolored original art design your children first draw on paper.

Above: Consider these storage solutions. Paint a flea market table and cover the front with your favorite fabric to hide clumsy, odd-shaped items that won't store easily on shelves. Search flea markets for shelving you can revitalize. Alternatively, buy unfinished shelves and paint them yourself—or have your children apply their own designs.

Opposite: Tuck a shelving box here and there for great little cubbies. Save money by purchasing unfinished furniture, then paint to match the room. Carry the theme of the room to the wall by cutting out a template from stiff cardboard, pinning it to the wall, tracing it, then painting away!

To make the carpeted area more interesting, talk to a carpet showroom manager about buying strips cut from other installations. Create a visually interesting carpeted section by mixing tweeds with stripes and primary colors.

Remember, too, that the playroom need not be cut in half. Divide it any way that makes sense. Make a quarter of the room a reading or quiet corner; install carpet in that area only. Another option is to paint a hardwood floor with a fun color, with a pattern of diamonds or stars, or with words that suggest activities for each area.

Walls

To save cleaning time and trouble, explore the following wallcover possibilities:

- **Blackboard paint:** Cover an entire wall, all four walls, a slice of wall, or the bottom half of all the walls in the room with blackboard paint, and give your children the freedom to express themselves.
- **Semigloss latex paint:** This is good for all the places little hands go—doors, window frames, and walls. A soapy sponge or window cleaner cleans this paint well.
- **Washable wallpaper:** Install this paper all around, or paint on the lower half and install wallpaper on top.

If your budget allows, hire an art student or a painter to create a cheery, interesting mural for the children to look at. This could work especially well if your playroom has no windows or poor light.

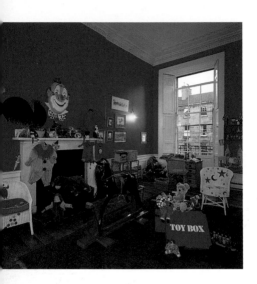

Above: There's no need to worry about fingerprints or sticky hands when walls are washable. Use semigloss paint or washable wallpaper. And do have fun! This bright red room, with clowns, big wooden farm animals, and painted furniture, would make any child feel welcome and happy.

Above: To brighten a room with too few windows, consider painting a scene on the walls. This works like wallpaper that tells a story and gives you and your child ideas to talk about. Note the padded toy box, great for little ones who could slam a finger or bump into the box.

Above: Even toddlers need a place to be creative, and in this room with kitties, flowers, and puppies on the fabric and wallpaper, it's easy to be artistically inspired!

Kids' Rooms

Furniture

When children are playing they move furniture and things around to suit their activities, so the lighter the better for playroom furnishings. Good choices include wicker, plastic, and air-filled furniture. Choose a style that fits the age group, and certainly consider bringing in that old sofa you were going to give away. Cover it with brightly colored sheets and let the children climb on it and play. If snacks or soda spill, you won't fret.

Another option is to buy big pillows and spread a few around the room.

Here's a list of playroom furniture to consider:

• child size chairs
• crafts table
• easel
• storage crates or baskets
• oversize pillows

Children love to play in enclosures, so, if you can, devote a portion of the room to a tent. Purchase a lightweight nylon tent from a camping store—it can be used both inside and outside—or fashion a simple tent from fabric. Some children's catalogs offer play tents, as well as flexible nylon crawl-through tubes and cardboard houses that can be colored with markers. Look through catalogs for playful ideas you might adapt and craft yourself.

Above: Here is a cheery playroom for toddlers. The lime-green painted wood, sunny papered walls, and the animal theme, from the curtains to the wall art, sets a fun mood.

Opposite: Children's outdoor play spaces can be as simple or elaborate as you wish. This amazing replica of a real house shows that our imagination, carpentry talents, time, and budget are our only limits!

Window Treatments

Keep window treatments simple and select easy-to-care-for solutions. If you want the ability to darken the room, shades are a good choice. Cover them with wallpaper or fabric that matches the room, or have a painting party with acrylics, and allow each of your children to design a shade. Another good option, if you sew, is to make café curtains to match a colorful fabric sheet you throw over the couch. If one side of the playroom is for paints, use vinyl curtains that would ordinarily be used in a child's bath.

If the room does not face the street, the children can make their own window decorations. For example, they could put a drawing in the bottom half of each window or paint a picture right on the glass (with the right paint, of course). They can use windowsills as display areas for their clay creations.

Outside Spaces

Finding Equipment

Many prefabricated exercise and play areas are available for backyard fun, as are tree house plans. An excellent way to research these is on the Internet, where you can view equipment and plans and correspond with the companies or, in some cases, with the actual designers. Search with your favorite search engine or library computer and look for the words "tree house" or "gym equipment" for a vast array of information. To check on the safest choices, do plenty of research, contact consumer safety groups, and consult parenting magazines before making the investment.

SITING A **PLAY AREA**

Kids love to be outdoors, pushing trucks through the sand or swinging high into the air. If you're going to have an outdoor swing set or sandbox, it's probably a good idea to site it under the shade of a tree to keep your children from the intense summer sun. This won't take the place of lotions, but it will help.

For toy storage, consider spray-painting a vinyl garbage bin bright red or yellow and placing it outside the back door. Make sure to buy one that your children can reach into easily. The bin will protect metal toys from rusting and keep other toys out of the elements as well.

As for the tree house, select a healthy tree with a good branch configuration to hold the structure. Height placement and access rights depend on the ages of your children.

Look for a level section of land in your yard, one that has good drainage as well. You don't want your sandbox sitting in a pool of soggy grass after a rainstorm.

Construct or buy a sandbox, or build a mock sandbox by edging a desired area with brick or a low metal sheet then fill that area with beach sand. Be careful if there are cats in the neighborhood; the sand will remind them of a litter box. If you do have cats nearby, a covered or gated sandbox will work best.

FURNISHING A **TREE HOUSE**

A tree house can provide a great escape and learning experience for kids. It gives them a space they can feel ownership over, and a tree house can teach them some of the responsibilities of adulthood—like keeping it clean. It can also encourage creativity, as the children can imagine the tree house as a remote castle or a secret hideaway. Read on for tips to make it feel a little more hospitable:

Simple ideas to decorate a tree house:

Cover old pillows or dog beds with washable fabric, and use as seats.

Make curtains from old sheets, blankets, towels, or pillowcases. Turn a hem, and for rods, use long sticks that rest on large cup rings and screw into the wall.

Have an art day when your children decorate. Use leftover wallpaper, paint, or floor tiles, and see how your kids integrate them here.

Cover the walls with snapshots of their friends or attach to a bulletin board you've hung here.

Try glow-in-the-dark stars or glow-in-the-dark paint on the ceiling.

To keep out mosquitoes, buy screen on a roll and staple it to the window frame. To liven things up, consider spray-painting the screen a fun color, and attaching paper bugs for atmosphere!

What can you put in a tree house? Here are a few suggestions your children may enjoy:

• an old blanket

• a board game or two that won't suffer in moisture

• a tin of hard candies

• a picnic basket for summertime lunches

• a disposable camera

• drawing supplies

• a plastic box for a few books and magazines

• suntan lotion

• bubble solution

• inexpensive binoculars and a bird book

• a butterfly net

• a flashlight

• bug repellent

• a guidebook to the planets and stars

• an inexpensive telescope

PET PLACES

If you have a dog or cat, or plan to, designing places for them to sit or perch is a good idea, as is thinking about the reality of their habits. Discuss with your children where the pet is allowed in your home, and how to best accommodate. In addition, you can design places for leashes, food, toys, and even litter storage, so that your children can participate in their care. Here are a few tips:

For the Dog

If you have a mudroom, or back door that your children frequently use to go outside with the pup, put a peg or hook for the leash at their height for easy access. In addition, consider adding a peg or hook that holds a vinyl bag for balls, and other dog toys. If there's room, add a third peg for a bag of edible treats.

Family dogs typically like to be with the family, and this usually means on the rug—not the easy-to-clean uncarpeted floor. If you leave the house, most often they sit and wait for you by the door. Consider placing a dark, richly patterned rug that won't show the hair or occasional wet paws. Or, put an extra bed there, over the rug; choose a fabric cover that complements the theme of the entry.

An option for dog food storage is a wicker hamper or closed wicker box that fits under an open counter at child height, or fits in the hall outside the kitchen. Or, you can create a family art project, and paint a wooden box—collage it with photos of your pet—and store in your kitchen. Do the same for treats!

When dogs come in from the rain, or snow, they need to be dried off. Make that your children's responsibility. Keep small, absorbent towels in the doorway in either a box or in a colorful pillowcase that you've strung with twine and hung on a peg.

Look around your house and see where else the dog tends to hang out, and add either a rich-colored, washable rug or another bed. Make your own pet bed cover to match the room or area, or put down a washable throw.

Cats

More than one pet owner holds the theory that the cat owns the house and simply allows the humans to visit. But, even though kitties go wherever they want to, you can make things that are helpful in cutting down on pet hair.

The simplest, and most attractive, is the common wicker basket lined with an old towel or blanket. Place one where the sun shines.

Ask your children to help you make the area even more attractive by selecting pretty fabric and crafting a simple cover for an old pillow. Try weaving ribbon in and out of the basket, or painting the outside in a cheerful hue that blends with the space.

If you notice, cats also like beds, or your favorite chair. Hem a pretty piece of fabric (with hem tape!), and place it on those spots to contain fur.

The food area—often a messy place—is another opportunity for kid-made crafts for pets: decorate a special placemat or two and use it to keep the feeding area tidy.

DECORATING TIPS
FROM THE KIDS

Aram

When 7-year-old Aram was asked to draw his favorite thing in his room, he drew his younger brother, Van. Asked what he would love to have in his room, he drew a window seat, and tossed in some books to illustrate what he would do there.

If his parents chose to construct a window seat because it would look good and worked with a redesign budget they had, perfect. Window seats, constructed as simple boxes that open, add storage and seating. A number of examples are shown in Chapter 3.

 If windows do not exist in number or at a height that accommodates a seat, hang a painting that depicts a window and outdoor scene. Alternatively, paint such a scene directly on the wall. Put a reading chair and bookshelf against it.

Instead of building a window seat, purchase a toy box or chest, cover it with a cushion, and place it in front of a window.

The thing I want is a window seat.

Aram

My favorite thing in my Room is Van my Brother.

Number 1, 2, 3, 4, 5, 5! he always sings this

Aram

Tommine

When Tommine's mom told her about my interest in having her draw her dream room, she took it as a special assignment. The 8½-year-old came to my house with detailed sketches in hand, prepared to color them while I watched. I quickly saw how much she wanted to communicate clearly what she loved. I couldn't help but smile at this trendy retro room.

Clearly, between 8 and 10, children begin to register fads and want to embrace them everywhere. The transition presages the jumps from 10 to 12 and 14 to 16, when individuality dramatically prevails! Consider how to anticipate these changes while accommodating present tastes.

Review these suggestions on working today's design preferences into a room while allowing convenient modification when the next trend hits:

- Cover the upper half of the walls with a bulletin board. Suggest that your child draw big illustrations of favorite things and pin them up.

- Paint the lower half of the wall a trendy color. This limits your investment to a gallon of purple paint, which can be inexpensively covered with the next popular shade.

- Buy unfinished furniture that can be painted and repainted quickly to accommodate changing tastes.

- Explore catalogs for moderately priced, trendy scatter rugs and bedcovers. The flower rug and smiley face are easy to find.

AT COOPER'S HOUSE

When Ann was pregnant with Cooper, she thought she would need to move her numerous collections—everything from birds' eggs to antique toys—to the safety of the attic of her dreamy 1800s sea captain's house. She was partially correct.

Kids' Rooms

In fact, before Cooper became a toddler, the collections comprised objects Ann and her husband, Chris, could point to and amuse, teach, or distract him with. The breakfast room, for example, is accented with bright colors and houses eggs and butterflies. Likewise, the bathroom on the second floor features a wicker chair full of seashells.

Now that Cooper can walk, some collections were moved to the attic for protection. To protect Cooper himself, gates were installed at the top and bottom of the stairs. The glass bookcase that held a collection of tin toys was retired to the attic; if Cooper pulled its knobs, the whole thing could crash. Chris advises parents to lay carpeting everywhere they can and install gates to avoid the injuries that come with inevitable falls.

Cooper's walker and swing bore him now now that he is walking. For his protection, sharp corners in the kitchen are padded. Thresholds may still trip him as he meanders from room to room, but he is proving more coordinated than Ann expected.

The distinctive decor—shabby chic and flea market finds—along with Chris' bad art collection, continues to stimulate Cooper as he walks. The fuss-free environment means he can play wherever he wishes. Perhaps there is a lesson here for all parents: Sprinkle colorful objects throughout your home as stimulating distractions for baby.

The original design idea for Cooper's bedroom was a cowboy or pirate theme, but his parents worried this was antiquated. Plain and colorful won out. Perhaps when he turns four, the room will be redone to reflect his developing interests and personality.

The walls are hand-painted by Ann, who traced a diamond grid all around the room. Cooper's crib is new, as are his dresser and bookcase. They were purchased unfinished and painted as well. Ann worried about lead paint, so she opted for painting everything herself. She might have been more apt to go for antique or flea market pieces normally, but she did not want to strip furniture while pregnant.

Ann did introduce one flea market find—an old rocker—recovering the seat pillow with Ralph Lauren fabric. The changing table, so temporary in a baby's life, was borrowed from a neighbor.

The bedroom's lack of closets called for some construction. Ann's father extended the wall at either side of the changing table and added closet doors. He put shelving and two rods in each, one for Cooper when he can hang his clothes and one at adult height.

When Cooper is older, he may graduate to the guest room across the hall, which is twice as big. Both rooms are near his parents'.

The bright yellow furnishings are cheery and provide a pleasing contrast to the soft colors of the diamonds. The lime-green curtains are made from bedsheets. The wall-to-wall carpeting is inexpensive; it was chosen to disappear into the decor. Its value is in function and safety.

MATERIALS

Canvas floor cloth, 2' x 3'
(.6 m x .9 m)

Masking tape

Ruler

Chalkboard finish, green

Expandable sponges, pack of 5

Scissors

Small plastic containers

Acrylic paints, Red, Blue, Yellow

Waxed paper

Sticky-back black felt squares

Chalk

OPTION:
TIC-TAC-TOE
PIECES

Polymer modeling clay,
two 2 oz. packages of each:
red, yellow, blue, green, and white

Glass baking dish

CRAFTING WITH KIDS

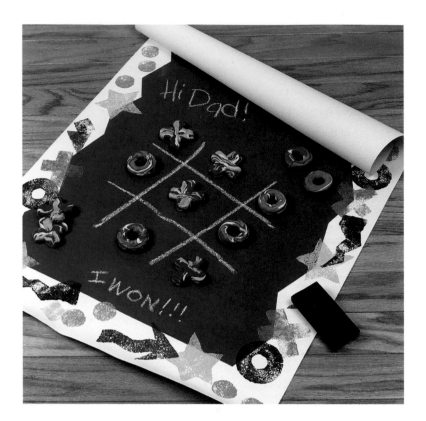

CHALKBOARD ROLL-UP

A perfect tool for a child's room or playroom with limited space, this chalkboard is perfect for drawing and practicing letters and numbers, or for special messages and great for car travel, too! Hang it on a wall or lay it on the floor. When you're finished, simply roll it up to store in a closet. Spray Chalkboard Finish makes this project possible. Simply spray the finish on a canvas floor cloth to create a fully erasable chalkboard surface. Then embellish your design with sponge-painted shapes. Materials make one chalkboard and one eraser. Double your fun by making polymer clay Xs and Os for hours of tic-tac-toe fun with your new chalkboard.

INSTRUCTIONS

1. Unroll the floor cloth and tape it down to a flat surface in a well-ventilated area. Use masking tape to mask off the area to be sprayed. Measure 3.5" (9 cm) in from each 2' (.6 m) side of the floor cloth, and tape a straight line (parallel to the edge of the canvas) to form the short sides of the rectangle. Then mask a random zig-zag design on each long side of the rectangle. Spray the Chalkboard Finish in several thin coats to avoid drips and puddles. Let dry, then remove the masking tape.

2. Trace simple shapes, such as stars, Xs, and Os, onto the compressed sponges. Cut out with scissors. Expand the sponges by running them under water, then let dry slightly. Mix paint colors in the small containers: yellow and blue for green; yellow and red for orange; and red and blue for purple. Spread some of all six colors (red, blue, yellow, green, orange and purple) onto waxed paper, and dip the sponge shapes into the paint. Wipe off any excess paint before stamping the shapes onto the border. Alternate and overlap your shapes to decorate the whole border.

3. Cut the self-stick felt into 12 equal pieces measuring 2" x 4.5" (5 cm x 11 cm). Put 2 pieces together (sticky side to sticky side) to create the bottom of the eraser. Then stack 9 more pieces (sticky side down) squarely on top of the original two. Cut the remaining 2" x 4.5" (5 cm x 11 cm) piece in half lengthwise, then trim 1" (3 cm) off of each end of one of those pieces. You will have one 1" x 4.5" (3 cm x 11 cm) piece and one 1" x 2.5" (3 cm x 6 cm) piece. Center the shorter piece on top of the longer piece, sticky side to sticky side. Then stick this new piece sticky side down to the top of the eraser, forming a handle.

OPTION: TIC-TAC-TOE PIECES

Instructions

1. For each O piece, take ¼ block of green clay, ¼ block of blue clay, and ⅛ block of white clay, and shape each into a short, fat, worm shape. Lay all three worms next to each other lengthwise. Twist the three worms together as the clay stretches. Fold the twisted worm in half and twist until you achieve a marbleized look. Shape the worm into an O.

2. To make an X, repeat the marbleizing process with ¼ block of yellow clay, ¼ block of red clay, and ⅛ block of white clay. When you have made your red, yellow, and white worm, form the worm into an X. Make six of each shape and bake them according to package directions.

TIPS

- Spray paint travels, so cover anything in the immediate area around the canvas. Read the directions on the can before spraying paint.

- When cutting out shapes from the sponge, use a craft knife to help cut out the center of the O.

- Save the sponge shapes for future art and crafts projects, or use them to decorate a playroom wall.

MATERIALS

Unfinished wooden stool,
14" x 10" x 11.5"
(36 cm x 25 cm x 29 cm)

Wood filler

Fine sandpaper

Paintbrush 1" (3 cm)

Acrylic paint, white

Stencil patterns (see pg. 134)

Glue

Lightweight cardboard

Craft knife

Colored pencils: orange,
magenta, turquoise,
green, yellow

Acrylic spray sealer, matte

Pencil sharpener

FUNKY FISH STOOL

This useful footstool combines a simple geometric design with
the fish pattern of your choice. Keep this stool near the sink for
little ones to wash up or in the playroom to reach books and
games on the upper shelves. Keep your pencils sharp and your
stencils lined up, and you can produce this decorated footstool
in a day! Simply paint the stool white. Then, use the patterns
provided to make your own stencils from cardboard. Use your
child's drawings to create your own design. Substitute elements
of your child's artwork for the patterns to create stencils that
include the images he prefers. This is a good place to use his
color choices, too, no matter how wild.

Kids' Rooms

INSTRUCTIONS

1. Fill any nail holes with wood filler, and let the filler dry. Lightly sand any rough spots and filled-in areas so that all the surfaces are smooth.

2. Slightly thin a small quantity of white paint with water. Paint this as a primer coat on the stool. Let it dry, and sand lightly all over. Apply a second coat of white paint, straight from the bottle, and let dry. If necessary, sand the second coat and apply a third coat.

3. Using the stencil patterns, glue them to lightweight cardboard, and cut out the designs using a craft knife. Place the triangle shapes along the edge of the top of the stool. Using a loose sketching motion, fill in the shapes with colored pencils: orange on the left, magenta on the right, and turquoise in the corners of the stool. Stencil a green circle above the turquoise corners. Following the photo, color in the fish stencil. Using the yellow pencil, color in circles in a random pattern on each side of the stool. Color in the hook and fly on the crosspiece.

4. Spray a light coat of acrylic sealer over the entire stool. After the first coat dries completely, spray several more light coats, allowing each coat to dry between applications.

TIP

• Be careful not to spray the sealer too heavily as this may cause dripping and the colors to run.

FUNKY FISH STOOL PATTERNS

Photocopy at 154%

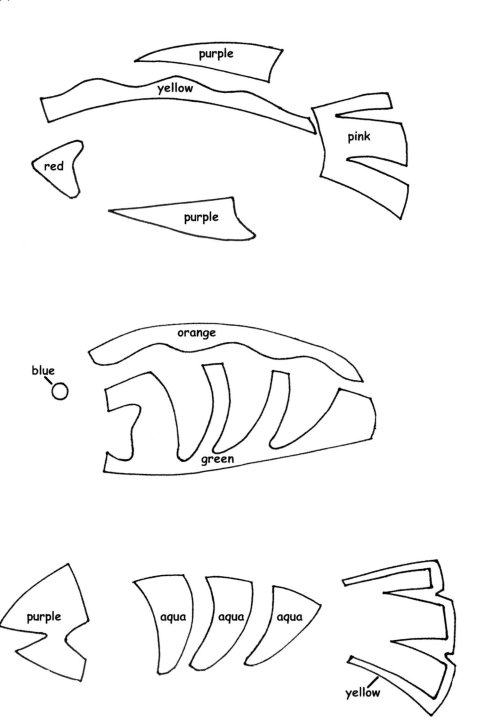

Photocopy at 133%

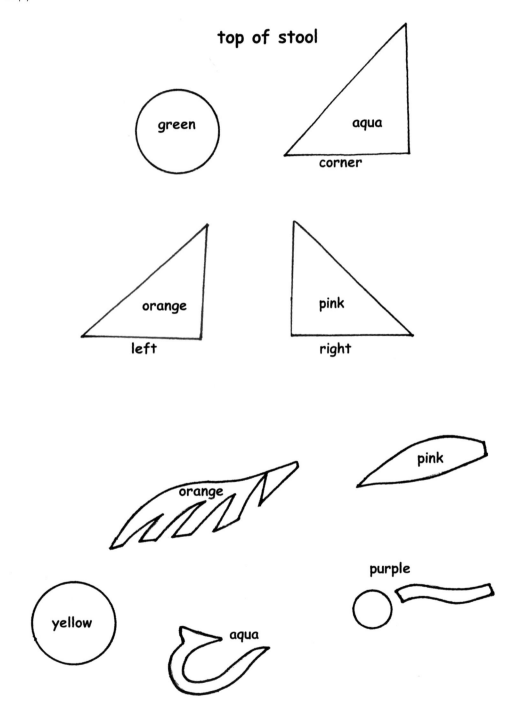

top of stool

green

aqua

corner

orange

left

pink

right

orange

pink

yellow

aqua

purple

RESOURCES FEATURED IN KIDS' ROOMS

Many of the designs for wallpapers, fabrics, and furnishings throughout the book come from the following companies:

Anna French Fabrics Ltd.
UK/Classic Revivals, Inc.,
exclusive U.S. agent
1 Design Center Place, Suite 534
Boston, MA 02210
Tel. 617-574-9030
Fax. 617-574-9027

Anna French Fabrics Ltd.
108 Shakespeare Road
London, S.E., 240QW
United Kingdom
Tel. 020-7737-9640
Fax. 020-7274-8913

Charm & Whimsy* *Ester*
114 East 32nd Street, Suite 603
NY, NY 10016
Tel. 212-683-7609

Laura Ashley, Inc.
6 Saint James Avenue
10th Floor, Boston, MA 02116
Tel. 617-457-6425
Fax. 617-457-6497

*See Decorating Tips from a Pro on page 26.

CATALOGS

These are catalogs I personally receive and go through regularly. All of them have items that will help you decorate. Please note that not all are specifically aimed at children, but you will find items appropriate for children's and family rooms.

Call these numbers to receive a catalog, or visit the web sites.

Anthropologie
800-543-1039
www.anthropologie.com

Charles Keath
800-388-6565
www.charleskeath.com

estyle.com/
babystyle.com/kidstyle.com
877-378-9537

Garnet Hill
800-622-6216

L'Art de Vivre
800-411-6515
www.indulge.com

Linensource
800-431-2620
www.linensource.com

Martha by Mail
800-950-7130
www.marthabymail.com

The Nature Company
800-227-1114

Neiman Marcus
800-825-8000
www.neimanmarcus.com

Pottery Barn
800-922-9934 or
800-922-5507

Shades of Light
800-262-6612

Sundance
800-422-2770
www.sundancecatalog.com

Windoware
800-248-8888

WEB SITES FOR CHILDREN'S ITEMS

You can see hundreds, maybe thousands of items, from cribs
to desks to lamps, at any of these web sites. Precede addresses
with www.

allwoodusa.com

amishmall.net

armsreach.com

babycyberstore.com

babygear.com

babyproductsonline.com

babystyle.com

bellini.com

bizrate.com

bunnies.com

calendarexpress.com

childwoodproducts.com

cozycreations.com

find-furniture.com

fingerhut.com

furniturechannel.com

furniturefan.com
*(Use this site to
search stores by zip
code and product.)*

grant.ent.com

guild.com

homeportfolio.com

iwillsave.com

kidcarpet.com

kidstation.com

kidstyle.com

littlebobbycreations.com

momastore.org

niftycool.com

productnetwork.com

ross-simons-online.com

seebuy.com

stores.suncommerce.com

storesearch.com

toyboxesetc.com

tuffyland.com

uniquehomegifts.com

PHOTO CREDITS

INDEX

DEDICATION

To my late mother, Katie, who nested so well, and Ellen, my friend since the fourth grade, whose bedroom was the one I wanted.

ACKNOWLEDGMENTS

My deepest thanks to Martha Wetherill, who saw this idea through to book form. I hope we do many more books together. Special thanks to the families and children in this book, my friend Nancy Klemm, who photographed many of them as they drew, and to Anna French/Classic Revivals, Inc. and Laura Ashley, Inc., whose work colors this book.

ABOUT THE **AUTHOR**

Anna Kasabian has written on numerous topics, including living, gardening, dining, traveling, and antiquing in New England, but her great passion is exploring modern interiors and architecturally significant homes, hotels, inns, and gardens. She is the author of *Designing Interiors with Tile: Creative Ideas with Ceramics, Stone, and Mosaic* and *East Coast Rooms.* As a contributor to *Cooking Spaces,* she explored the at-home kitchens of some of the most respected chefs and food writers in here and abroad. Her byline frequently appears in the *Boston Globe,* where she writes about homes and gardens. In addition, she writes for *Woman's Day, Boston Magazine,* and *New England Travel and Life.* She scouts and produces for HGTV and has appeared on the popular show Bed and Bath Design for the Home and Garden channel as well.